Switzerland Travel Guide 2025

Discover Switzerland's Top Attractions, Hidden Gems, Cultural Highlights, Timely Itineraries, and Budget-Friendly Hacks for Every Traveler

Janie Moreno

Switzerland Travel Guide 2025`

Copyright Notice

No part of this book may be reproduced, written, electronic, recorded, or photocopied without written permission from the publisher or author.

The exception would be in the case of brief quotations embodied in critical articles or reviews and pages where permission is specifically granted by the publisher or author.

Although every precaution has been taken to verify the accuracy of the information contained herein, the author and publisher assume no responsibility for any errors or omissions. No liability is assumed for damages that may result from the use of the information contained within.

All Rights Reserved ©2025 Janie Moreno

Switzerland Travel Guide 2025`

TABLE OF CONTENT

INTRODUCTION	**11**
WELCOME TO SWITZERLAND	12
WHY VISIT SWITZERLAND IN 2025?	13
HOW TO USE THIS GUIDE	14
TRAVEL TRENDS AND INSIGHTS FOR 2025	16
CHAPTER 1: PLANNING YOUR TRIP TO SWITZERLAND	**19**
WHEN TO VISIT: BEST SEASONS AND MONTHS	19
BUDGETING FOR YOUR TRIP TO SWITZERLAND	22
HOW MANY DAYS DO YOU NEED?	24
VISA REQUIREMENTS & ENTRY REGULATIONS (2025 UPDATE)	25
TRAVEL INSURANCE TIPS	26
SWISS PASS & OTHER TRANSPORT CARDS	28
CHAPTER 2: GETTING TO SWITZERLAND	**31**
MAJOR INTERNATIONAL AIRPORTS IN SWITZERLAND	31
DIRECT FLIGHTS FROM KEY GLOBAL CITIES	32
TRAIN TRAVEL FROM NEIGHBORING COUNTRIES	34
CUSTOMS & IMMIGRATION TIPS	35
CHAPTER 3: GETTING AROUND SWITZERLAND	**37**
SWISS RAIL NETWORK OVERVIEW	37
DRIVING IN SWITZERLAND	39
PUBLIC TRANSPORTATION IN CITIES	40
SCENIC TRAIN JOURNEYS (GLACIER EXPRESS, BERNINA EXPRESS, ETC.)	42
BIKE RENTALS AND WALKING TRAILS	44

Switzerland Travel Guide 2025`

CHAPTER 4: WHERE TO STAY IN SWITZERLAND — 47

TOP CITIES AND REGIONS FOR ACCOMMODATION — 47
LUXURY HOTELS & RESORTS — 50
MID-RANGE OPTIONS — 59
BUDGET STAYS & HOSTELS — 67
BOOKING TIPS FOR 2025 — 72

CHAPTER 5: TOP DESTINATIONS IN SWITZERLAND — 77

ZURICH: FINANCIAL CAPITAL MEETS CULTURE — 77
GENEVA: INTERNATIONAL FLAVOR BY THE LAKE — 78
LUCERNE: MEDIEVAL CHARM AND LAKE VIEWS — 80
BERN: UNESCO-LISTED CAPITAL — 81
LAUSANNE: CULTURE & VINEYARDS — 83
BASEL: ART, ARCHITECTURE & RHINE RIVER — 84
INTERLAKEN: GATEWAY TO THE ALPS — 86
ZERMATT: HOME OF THE MATTERHORN — 87
LUGANO: SWISS-MEDITERRANEAN CHARM — 89

CHAPTER 6: TOP ATTRACTION IN SWITZERLAND — 91

THE MATTERHORN — 91
LAKE GENEVA — 94
THE JUNGFRAU REGION — 97
CHÂTEAU DE CHILLON — 99
INTERLAKEN — 101
LUCERNE AND LAKE LUCERNE — 103
THE SWISS NATIONAL PARK — 105
ZURICH — 107

Switzerland Travel Guide 2025`

CHAPTER 7: NATURAL WONDERS AND LANDSCAPES — 109

The Swiss Alps: Hiking, Skiing, and Panoramas — 109
Iconic Mountains: Matterhorn, Eiger, and Jungfrau — 110
Lakes of Switzerland: Geneva, Lucerne, Zurich, and More — 112
Waterfalls, Gorges, and Caves — 113
National Parks and Nature Reserves — 116

CHAPTER 8: SWISS CULTURE AND TRADITIONS — 117

Languages and Regional Difference — 117
Swiss Festivals and Events (2025 Calendar) — 119
Alpine Folklore and Music — 121
Traditional Clothing and Customs — 122
Understanding Swiss Neutrality and Civic Pride — 124

CHAPTER 9: OUTDOOR ADVENTURES AND ACTIVITIES — 127

Skiing & Snowboarding Resorts — 127
Hiking Trails and Alpine Routes — 129
Paragliding, Ziplining, and Skydiving — 130
Mountain Biking and Climbing — 132
Winter vs Summer Activities — 133
Mountain Biking and Climbing — 135
Winter vs Summer Activities — 137

CHAPTER 10: FOOD AND DRINK IN SWITZERLAND — 139

Traditional Swiss Cuisine — 139
Must-Try Dishes: Fondue, Rösti, Raclette, and More — 147
Swiss Chocolate and Cheese — 149
Wine Regions and Vineyards — 151
Best Restaurants by Region — 153

CHAPTER 11: 7-DAY ULTIMATE SWITZERLAND ADVENTURE — 157

DAY 1: ARRIVAL IN ZURICH & EXPLORE THE CITY	157
DAY 2: DAY TRIP TO LUCERNE	159
DAY 3: TRAVEL TO INTERLAKEN & ADVENTURE ACTIVITIES	162
DAY 4: JUNGFRAUJOCH – TOP OF EUROPE	164
DAY 5: ZERMATT & MATTERHORN VIEWS	165
DAY 6: GLACIER EXPRESS & CHUR	167
DAY 7: DEPARTURE FROM ZURICH	169

CHAPTER 12: SUSTAINABLE AND RESPONSIBLE TRAVEL — 171

ECO-FRIENDLY TRANSPORTATION	171
GREEN HOTELS AND LODGES	172
SUPPORTING LOCAL COMMUNITIES	174
WASTE MANAGEMENT AND RECYCLING IN SWITZERLAND	175
ETHICAL OUTDOOR PRACTICES	176

CHAPTER 13: SHOPPING IN SWITZERLAND — 179

SWISS WATCHES AND TIMEPIECES	179
CHOCOLATE, CHEESE, AND GOURMET GIFTS	180
LOCAL ARTISANS AND CRAFT MARKETS	182
HIGH-END BOUTIQUES AND LUXURY GOODS	183
VAT REFUND AND SHOPPING TIPS	184

CHAPTER 14: PRACTICAL INFORMATION AND TRAVEL TIPS — 187

CURRENCY, BANKING, AND CREDIT CARDS	187
HEALTH & SAFETY ADVICE	188
INTERNET, SIM CARDS, AND CONNECTIVITY	190
USEFUL APPS FOR TRAVEL IN SWITZERLAND	192
EMERGENCY NUMBERS & CONTACTS	194

SWISS ETIQUETTE AND DOS & DON'TS	195
BONUS 1: SWITZERLAND ON A BUDGET	**198**
HOW TO TRAVEL SWITZERLAND CHEAPLY	199
FREE ATTRACTIONS & SCENIC SPOTS	201
AFFORDABLE EATS: WHERE LOCALS DINE	203
BEST BUDGET HOTELS & HOSTELS	204
HOW TO MAXIMIZE THE SWISS TRAVEL PASS	206
BONUS 2: HIDDEN GEMS OF SWITZERLAND	**208**
SECRET VILLAGES WITH STUNNING VIEWS	209
OFF-THE-RADAR LAKES & TRAILS	211
LOCAL CAFÉS, MARKETS & ARTISAN SHOPS	212
PEACEFUL ALTERNATIVES TO BUSY CITIES	214
LESSER-KNOWN FESTIVALS WORTH ATTENDING	215
BONUS 3: SWISS TRAVEL MISTAKES TO AVOID	**216**
MOST COMMON TOURIST TRAPS	217
MONEY-WASTING MISTAKES	220
TRANSPORTATION PITFALLS	222
CULTURAL MISSTEPS TO AVOID	224
WHAT TO PACK (AND WHAT TO LEAVE BEHIND)	227
BONUS 4: SWITZERLAND TRAVEL ITINERARIES	**230**
ROMANTIC 5-DAY GETAWAY	231
FAMILY-FRIENDLY WEEK IN THE ALPS	234
FOOD & WINE LOVER'S TOUR	237
ADVENTURE SEEKER'S 7-DAY ROUTE	240

THE SCENIC PHOTOGRAPHER'S DREAM TRIP	**243**
BONUS 5: SWISS PHRASES FOR TRAVELERS	**246**
MUST-KNOW WORDS IN GERMAN, FRENCH & ITALIAN	247
HOW TO ORDER FOOD & ASK FOR DIRECTIONS	251
POLITE PHRASES FOR BETTER CONNECTIONS	253
TRAIN, HOTEL & RESTAURANT VOCABULARY	254
FUN LOCAL EXPRESSIONS TOURISTS LOVE	255

Switzerland Travel Guide 2025`

Switzerland Travel Guide 2025`

Switzerland Travel Guide 2025`

INTRODUCTION

Are you overwhelmed by the thought of planning a trip to Switzerland? Wondering how to make the most of your time in this stunning yet expensive country? Do you struggle with choosing the best time to visit, finding affordable accommodations, or navigating Switzerland's efficient but intricate transportation system? How can you enjoy the breathtaking beauty of the Alps without breaking the bank? Are you curious about Swiss culture but unsure how to experience it authentically?

If these questions have crossed your mind, you're not alone. Switzerland is one of the most enchanting destinations in the world, but its pristine beauty and high standards can make travel planning feel like a challenge. Whether you're a luxury traveler, a budget-conscious explorer, or someone seeking off-the-beaten-path experiences, planning a trip can be intimidating.

But fear not. This *Switzerland Travel Guide 2025* is designed to take the guesswork out of your travel plans. From the best seasons to visit to budget-friendly tips, this guide covers everything you need to know to make your Swiss adventure unforgettable. Whether you're exploring the medieval streets of Lucerne, hiking the Alps, or tasting world-famous Swiss chocolate, we've got you covered with detailed itineraries, local secrets, and practical advice.

Inside, you'll find:

- Seasonal recommendations and expert tips to save you money.
- A breakdown of must-see cities, attractions, and hidden gems.
- Insider knowledge on Swiss culture, food, and traditions.
- Fun and thrilling outdoor activities, from skiing in the Alps to paragliding over Interlaken.
- Sustainable travel practices, so you can enjoy Switzerland responsibly.

So, whether you're planning a short getaway or a week-long adventure, this guide will help you craft the ultimate Swiss experience—without the stress. Let's dive in and start planning the trip of a lifetime!

Welcome to Switzerland

A land where snow-capped mountains meet crystal-clear lakes, where charming alpine villages coexist with cosmopolitan cities, and where every train ride feels like a journey through a postcard—Switzerland is more than a destination; it's an experience.

From the towering Matterhorn to the serene shores of Lake Geneva, from the bustling streets of Zurich to the peaceful trails of the Bernese Oberland, this country offers something for every kind of traveler. Whether you're seeking outdoor adventure, cultural immersion, gourmet delights, or simply the joy of slow travel through stunning landscapes, Switzerland delivers it all—effortlessly.

This guide will be your companion as you explore not just the famous landmarks, but also the hidden corners, local traditions, and authentic stories that make Switzerland truly unforgettable.

Welcome to a journey filled with breathtaking beauty, timeless charm, and unforgettable moments.

Welcome to Switzerland.

Why Visit Switzerland in 2025?

Switzerland is a destination that consistently draws travelers from around the world, and 2025 is the perfect time to experience all that this stunning country has to offer. With its awe-inspiring landscapes, rich cultural heritage, and world-class amenities, there are countless reasons to make Switzerland your next travel destination. Here's why you should consider visiting Switzerland in 2025:

Unmatched Natural Beauty: The Swiss Alps are iconic, offering breathtaking views that will leave you speechless. From hiking trails to snow-capped peaks and tranquil lakes, Switzerland's landscapes are perfect for nature lovers and outdoor enthusiasts alike.

Sustainable Tourism: As a global leader in environmental conservation, Switzerland continues to make strides in eco-friendly tourism. Whether you're hiking in the Swiss National Park or using public transportation, you can explore the country while minimizing your environmental footprint.

Year-Round Adventures: Whether you're into skiing and snowboarding during the winter months or hiking and mountain biking in the summer, Switzerland offers a year-round adventure for every type of traveler. The range of seasonal activities makes it a versatile destination for any time of year.

Rich Culture & Heritage: Switzerland's deep cultural roots span centuries, and 2025 promises to be an exciting year for those wanting to dive into its unique traditions. Explore UNESCO-listed sites, medieval towns, and modern cities that blend the old and new seamlessly.

Culinary Delights: Swiss cuisine is a delicious mix of French, Italian, and German influences, with famous dishes like fondue, raclette, and Rösti. Swiss chocolate, cheeses, and wines are world-renowned, offering foodies a true taste of luxury and authenticity.

Effortless Travel: Switzerland's highly efficient public transportation system makes it easy to explore every corner of the country. With scenic train journeys like the Glacier Express and Bernina Express, traveling through Switzerland is as much a part of the experience as the destinations themselves.

Top-Tier Safety & Hospitality: Switzerland is known for its safety, cleanliness, and exceptional hospitality. Whether you're in a bustling city or a quiet mountain village, you'll feel welcomed and cared for throughout your journey.

Switzerland Travel Guide 2025`

Festivals and Events: In 2025, Switzerland will host numerous cultural events, festivals, and celebrations. From art exhibitions in Basel to music festivals in Geneva, there's no shortage of exciting happenings that will immerse you in the country's vibrant cultural scene.

New Experiences and Innovations: With continuous developments in tourism infrastructure, Switzerland is introducing even more exciting ways to experience its beauty, from luxury wellness resorts to cutting-edge technology in eco-tourism.

In short, 2025 is the ideal time to visit Switzerland for its spectacular natural landscapes, rich cultural offerings, and an ever-evolving tourism scene that promises new adventures for every type of traveler. Whether you're seeking relaxation, adventure, or cultural immersion, Switzerland will captivate your heart and soul.

How to Use This Guide

Whether you're a first-time visitor or returning to Switzerland to uncover more of its charm, this guide is designed to be your trusted companion every step of the way. To make your travel planning effortless and your journey unforgettable, here's how to get the most out of this book:

Start with the Basics

Begin with **Chapter 1: Planning Your Trip to Switzerland**. This section helps you decide the best time to visit, how long to stay, what to budget, and what essential documents you'll need. It's your foundation for a smooth, stress-free trip.

Choose How You'll Arrive and Move Around

Chapters 2 and 3 walk you through getting to and navigating within Switzerland. Learn about major airports, train routes from neighboring countries, scenic rail journeys, and local transportation options. This section is especially useful if you plan to rely on Switzerland's world-class public transit system.

Pick Where to Stay

Turn to **Chapter 4** to explore your accommodation options, from luxury resorts to budget hostels. Whether you're a solo traveler, couple, family, or group, you'll find tips on where to stay that match your style and budget.

Discover the Best Places to Visit

Dive into **Chapters 5 and 6** for a breakdown of Switzerland's top cities and must-see attractions. These chapters give you a curated overview of what each destination offers—perfect for building your itinerary.

Explore Beyond the Tourist Trail

Chapter 7 focuses on natural wonders and landscapes, while **Chapter 8** dives into Swiss culture and traditions. Use these chapters to connect more deeply with the places you visit, whether it's through nature, history, or local customs.

Plan Outdoor Adventures

If you're craving adrenaline or fresh alpine air, **Chapter 9** details outdoor activities, from skiing and hiking to skydiving and biking. This chapter is your gateway to adventure, regardless of the season.

Savor the Flavors of Switzerland

Chapter 10 introduces you to Swiss food and drink, from iconic dishes to local wine regions. Whether you're dining out or sampling chocolate, this section will enhance your culinary journey.

Follow a Ready-Made Itinerary

Short on time or overwhelmed by options? **Chapter 11** offers a detailed 7-day itinerary that highlights Switzerland's best, balancing adventure, relaxation, and scenic travel.

Travel Responsibly

Chapter 12 focuses on sustainable and responsible travel. Learn how to enjoy Switzerland while supporting local communities and protecting its pristine environment.

Shop and Travel Smart

Use **Chapter 13** for tips on shopping for authentic Swiss goods like watches, chocolate, and cheese. **Chapter 14** provides practical advice on money, connectivity, health, etiquette, and more.

Switzerland Travel Guide 2025`

Pro Tip: This guide is designed to be both linear and flexible. Feel free to skip directly to the sections that matter most to you. Whether you're planning months in advance or flipping through on the train to your next destination, every chapter is packed with actionable, up-to-date insights.

Travel Trends and Insights for 2025

As global travel continues to evolve, 2025 brings forth a blend of innovation, sustainability, and personalization. Travelers are seeking deeper connections, meaningful experiences, and value-driven choices. Here are the top travel trends shaping the year:

1. Sustainable and Eco-Conscious Travel

Environmental awareness is at the forefront of travelers' minds. There's a significant shift towards sustainable tourism, with travelers opting for:

Certified eco-friendly accommodations

Low-emission transportation options

Flight-free getaways closer to home

Transparency in sustainability practices

This trend is particularly strong among Gen Z and Millennials, who prioritize minimizing their environmental footprint while exploring new destinations.

2. Rise of Solo and Wellness Travel

Solo travel continues to gain momentum, with a focus on self-care and personal growth. Travelers are seeking experiences that offer relaxation, wellness, and introspection. This includes retreats centered around:

Mindfulness and meditation

Spa and wellness treatments

Nature immersion and digital detoxes

The emphasis is on journeys that rejuvenate the mind and body, catering to the growing demand for wellness-centric vacations.

3. Flexible and Hybrid Travel Experiences

The concept of "flexiscapes" is emerging, where travelers blend adventure with relaxation. This approach involves starting a trip with budget-friendly, activity-rich experiences and concluding with indulgent luxury stays. It allows travelers to maximize their budgets while enjoying a diverse range of experiences.

4. Cultural Immersion and Educational Travel

Travelers are seeking deeper cultural connections and educational experiences. There's a growing interest in:

Visiting museums and historical sites with a focus on underrepresented narratives

Participating in local workshops and community projects

Exploring destinations through the lens of social and historical contexts

This trend reflects a desire for meaningful engagement and a better understanding of diverse cultures.

5. Family-Centric and Child-Inclusive Travel

Family vacations are becoming more collaborative, with children actively participating in planning. This approach leads to unique and memorable experiences tailored to the interests of all family members. Activities range from unconventional dining experiences to educational adventures, fostering stronger family bonds and lifelong memories.

6. Economic Considerations and Value-Driven Choices

Economic uncertainties are influencing travel behaviors. Travelers are becoming more cost-conscious, seeking value without compromising on experience. This includes:

Shorter booking windows

Preference for budget-friendly accommodations

Utilizing travel hacks and loyalty programs

Despite these considerations, the desire for travel remains strong, with a focus on maximizing experiences within budget constraints.

7. Growth of Cruise Tourism

While air travel faces challenges, the cruise industry is experiencing a resurgence. Cruises offer:

All-inclusive packages providing value for money

Diverse itineraries catering to various interests

Enhanced health and safety measures

The convenience and comprehensive nature of cruises are attracting travelers seeking hassle-free vacation options.

8. Emphasis on Sleep and Restorative Travel

Sleep tourism is gaining traction, focusing on rest and rejuvenation. Travelers are opting for accommodations and experiences that prioritize:

High-quality sleep environments

Wellness programs targeting sleep improvement

Destinations known for tranquility and natural beauty

This trend underscores the importance of rest in overall well-being and the desire for vacations that restore energy and vitality.

Switzerland Travel Guide 2025`

Chapter 1: Planning Your Trip to Switzerland

When to Visit: Best Seasons and Months

Switzerland's diverse geography offers a unique experience depending on the season, with dramatic contrasts between the snow-covered Alps in winter and lush green landscapes in the summer. Deciding when to visit depends on your interests, but here's a breakdown of each season to help you choose the best time for your trip:

Winter (December to February) – A Snowy Wonderland

Ideal For: Skiing, snowboarding, and winter sports lovers.

What to Expect: Switzerland's winter is magical, with snow blanketing the Alps and picturesque towns. Major ski resorts like Zermatt, St. Moritz, and Verbier are bustling with visitors. In cities, Christmas markets light up streets, and cozy chalets offer a quintessential winter experience.

Key Highlights:

Skiing & Snowboarding: The Swiss Alps are famous for some of the best skiing and snowboarding in the world. Whether you're a beginner or an expert, resorts offer a range of slopes.

Winter Sports Festivals: Attend snow festivals, ice-skating events, and thrilling competitions like the Engadine Ski Marathon.

Christmas Markets: Explore festive markets in Zurich, Lucerne, and Basel, offering local crafts, Swiss chocolate, mulled wine, and seasonal delicacies.

Best Months to Visit: December through February are peak months for winter sports. However, early December can be quieter and more affordable before the holiday rush.

Spring (March to May) – Awakening Nature

Ideal For: Hiking, sightseeing, and fewer crowds.

Switzerland Travel Guide 2025`

What to Expect: Spring is a quieter, more peaceful time in Switzerland. The Alps start to shed their snow, wildflowers bloom across valleys, and the weather begins to warm up. While the ski season is winding down, it's the perfect time for hiking, especially in lower-altitude regions.

Key Highlights:

Wildflower Season: Hiking trails in regions like the Swiss National Park or the Lauterbrunnen Valley are adorned with wildflowers.

Mild Weather: This is a great time to visit cities, enjoy lakefront strolls, or take scenic train rides through the Alps.

Spring Festivals: Experience events like the Geneva Festival or the Zürich Spring Fair, where locals celebrate the season with music, food, and crafts.

Best Months to Visit: April and May are ideal for those looking to avoid peak crowds. The weather is mild, and the attractions are less busy than in the summer months.

Summer (June to August) – Vibrant and Lush

Ideal For: Outdoor enthusiasts, hikers, and those seeking cultural experiences.

What to Expect: Switzerland in summer is at its most vibrant. The Alps are accessible for hiking, cycling, and outdoor activities. The lakesides are perfect for swimming or boating, and major cities come alive with festivals, outdoor dining, and cultural events.

Key Highlights:

Alpine Hiking: Switzerland offers some of Europe's best hiking trails, with options for all levels. Trek the famous Matterhorn or Jungfrau regions, or try the scenic Gotthard Pass.

Mountain Biking and Paragliding: For adrenaline lovers, Switzerland's mountains provide world-class biking and paragliding opportunities.

Lake Activities: Enjoy boat rides on Lake Geneva, Lake Lucerne, or Lake Zurich. Summer is ideal for relaxing by the water, picnicking, or taking a leisurely boat tour.

Festivals: The Montreux Jazz Festival, Locarno Film Festival, and the Fête de l'Escalade in Geneva are just a few of the many events that draw both locals and tourists.

Best Months to Visit: June through August are the peak summer months, with warm temperatures (around 20–30°C or 68–86°F). These months are ideal for hiking, outdoor activities, and cultural festivals.

Autumn (September to November) – A Tranquil Retreat

Ideal For: Autumn foliage, photography, and wine enthusiasts.

What to Expect: As the leaves turn golden and the weather cools, Switzerland's autumn months bring stunning colors to its landscapes. The summer crowds begin to thin, making it a peaceful time to explore. Many regions, especially in the south, harvest grapes for wine, and you'll see vineyards at their most picturesque.

Key Highlights:

Autumn Foliage: The trees around lakes and valleys, particularly in the Engadine and Ticino regions, burst with color, making it one of the best times for nature lovers and photographers.

Wine Harvesting: In the Canton of Valais and other wine regions, autumn is harvest time. Visit vineyards for wine tastings and special harvest tours.

Cultural Events: Festivals like the Zurich Film Festival and the Basel Autumn Fair are excellent cultural experiences.

Best Months to Visit: Late September through November is ideal for those who prefer cooler temperatures, fewer crowds, and the beauty of autumn's changing leaves.

Budgeting for Your Trip to Switzerland

Switzerland is known for its high quality of life, but this comes with a price tag. However, with careful planning, it is possible to explore this beautiful country on a budget. Here are some key strategies for budgeting your Swiss trip effectively:

1. Accommodation Costs

Luxury Hotels: The top-tier accommodations in Switzerland can be quite pricey, with five-star hotels in cities like Zurich, Geneva, and Lucerne charging upwards of CHF 300–500 per night. In ski resorts, the prices can even go higher during peak seasons.

Mid-Range Hotels: For more affordable yet comfortable options, consider mid-range hotels, guesthouses, or boutique hotels. Expect to pay around CHF 150–250 per night.

Budget Stays: Hostels, guesthouses, or Airbnb rentals can offer more affordable options, especially if you book in advance. Expect to pay CHF 50–100 per night for a shared room or budget-friendly private rooms.

Camping: Switzerland offers a wealth of camping opportunities, particularly in rural or alpine regions. Campsites and caravan parks range from CHF 25–50 per night, making it a great low-cost option for outdoor lovers.

2. Transportation

Swiss Travel Pass: For travelers planning to explore the country by train, the Swiss Travel Pass offers unlimited travel on the Swiss Travel System network, including trains, buses, and boats. The pass also covers free entry to museums. Prices vary by duration: 3-day passes start at CHF 213.

Trains & Public Transport: Switzerland's rail system is efficient and well-connected. For those not using a Swiss Travel Pass, tickets between cities generally range from CHF 30–100, depending on distance. Public transportation in cities (trams, buses, etc.) costs around CHF 2–5 per ride.

Car Rentals: While renting a car offers flexibility, it can be expensive. Rental prices start around CHF 60 per day, and parking fees in major cities can add up. It's important to check local parking availability and fees.

Bike Rentals: Many Swiss cities have bike-sharing programs, and bike rentals cost between CHF 20–50 per day, making it a great way to explore at a lower cost.

3. Dining & Food Costs

Restaurants: Dining in Switzerland can be expensive, particularly in major cities or tourist hotspots. A meal at a mid-range restaurant typically costs CHF 25–50 per person. Opt for lunch menus, which are often cheaper.

Street Food & Takeaways: For a more budget-friendly option, look for street food stalls or takeaway food, where prices are usually CHF 10–20 for quick bites like sandwiches, pizza, or Swiss sausages.

Supermarkets: To save on meals, consider shopping at local supermarkets like Coop or Migros. Prepared meals, sandwiches, and snacks are available at reasonable prices (CHF 5–15). This is a great option for picnics or casual dining.

Swiss Chocolate & Cheese: Don't miss out on Switzerland's world-famous chocolate and cheese. Purchasing these as souvenirs is affordable, with prices ranging from CHF 5–30 depending on the selection.

4. Activities and Attractions

Free Activities: Switzerland offers many free activities, especially in nature. Hiking, swimming in lakes, and exploring charming villages are all free options that allow you to experience the country without breaking the bank.

Museums & Attractions: Entrance fees for museums and attractions typically range from CHF 10–25. Many museums offer discounts or free entry on certain days of the month, so be sure to check in advance.

Tourist Passes: In cities like Zurich and Lucerne, you can purchase a city pass for CHF 30–50 that grants discounted or free entry to multiple attractions, as well as unlimited use of public transport.

5. Saving Tips

Plan in Advance: Book accommodation, transportation, and some popular attractions ahead of time to get the best deals.

Travel Off-Peak: Traveling outside peak seasons (especially summer and winter holidays) can save you money on flights, accommodation, and activities.

Look for Package Deals: Consider booking multi-day packages that include transport, accommodation, and meals, as they can offer significant savings compared to booking each separately.

Use a Travel Credit Card: Many travel credit cards offer rewards, free international transactions, or points that can help reduce the cost of your trip.

Estimated Daily Budget (Per Person)

Budget Traveler: CHF 100–150

Mid-Range Traveler: CHF 150–300

Luxury Traveler: CHF 300–500+

With a little planning and flexibility, Switzerland can be enjoyed without overspending, offering a combination of spectacular landscapes, rich culture, and unique experiences that are well worth the investment.

How Many Days Do You Need?

The ideal duration for your Swiss adventure depends on your interests, pace, and the regions you wish to explore. Here's a breakdown to help you plan:

Short Trip (3–4 days): Ideal for a quick city tour. You can explore Zurich, Lucerne, and Interlaken, experiencing urban culture, lakeside views, and a taste of the Alps.

Classic Itinerary (7 days): A balanced mix of cities and nature. Visit Zurich, Lucerne, Interlaken, and Zermatt, with scenic train journeys like the Glacier Express.

Extended Exploration (10–14 days): For those wanting to delve deeper, include Geneva, Bern, Lausanne, and the Italian-speaking region of Ticino. This allows for more leisurely exploration and immersion in Swiss culture.

Remember, Switzerland's efficient public transport system makes it feasible to explore multiple regions in a relatively short time.

Visa Requirements & Entry Regulations (2025 Update)

Switzerland is part of the **Schengen Area**, though it is not a member of the European Union (EU). Entry rules and visa requirements are governed by Schengen regulations, with some specific national nuances. Here's what you need to know for 2025:

1. Who Needs a Visa?

Visa-Free Countries: Citizens from over 60 countries—including the **USA, UK, Canada, Australia, Japan, South Korea**, and most countries in South America—**do not need a visa** for short stays of up to **90 days within a 180-day period**.

Visa Required Countries: Travelers from many parts of Africa, Asia, and the Middle East must apply for a **Schengen Visa (Type C)** before arrival.

2. ETIAS Launch (New in 2025)

Starting **mid-2025**, the **European Travel Information and Authorization System (ETIAS)** will become mandatory for **visa-exempt travelers**.

ETIAS is **not a visa**, but an electronic travel authorization similar to the U.S. ESTA.

You'll need to apply online before your trip, providing personal data, travel details, and a small fee (approx. €7). Once approved, ETIAS is valid for **three years** or until your passport expires.

This applies to **non-EU, visa-free countries**, including Americans, Brits, Australians, etc.

3. Schengen Visa (For Those Who Need It)

Apply at the **Swiss embassy or consulate** in your home country.

Typical documents include:

Completed application form

Valid passport (with at least 3 months' validity post-return)

Proof of travel insurance (see next section)

Round-trip flight reservation

Accommodation details

Proof of financial means

Visa fee (approx. €80)

Processing Time: Apply at least **15 days to 3 months** before your intended travel date.

4. Entry Requirements at the Border

Even if you don't need a visa, **border officials may ask to see**:

Return or onward ticket

Proof of accommodation (hotel booking, invitation letter, etc.)

Proof of sufficient funds (bank statements, credit cards, etc.)

Valid travel insurance covering the Schengen zone

5. COVID-19 and Health Regulations (as of 2025)

Switzerland currently has **no COVID-related entry restrictions**, but travelers should check closer to their departure in case of new developments or public health advisories.

Travel Insurance Tips

Travel insurance is **strongly recommended** and often **mandatory** (especially if you require a visa). Here's what you need to consider when choosing coverage for your trip to Switzerland in 2025:

1. Is Travel Insurance Required?

Mandatory for Schengen Visa applicants: Your policy must cover at least €30,000 for medical expenses, hospitalization, and repatriation.

Highly recommended for everyone else, especially given Switzerland's high cost of healthcare and activities like skiing, hiking, or adventure sports.

2. What Should Your Policy Cover?

Look for a comprehensive plan that includes:

Medical Expenses: Emergency treatment, hospitalization, medication.

Emergency Evacuation & Repatriation: Costs to transport you home or to another facility.

Trip Cancellation/Interruption: Reimbursement for non-refundable bookings if your trip is delayed, interrupted, or canceled.

Lost/Stolen Luggage & Personal Items: Especially useful for high-value items or delayed baggage.

Adventure Sports Coverage: If you plan to ski, paraglide, or hike in high-altitude terrain, you'll need an *add-on* or specific *adventure policy*.

Travel Delay & Missed Connection: To help with costs if delays occur due to weather or strikes.

3. Special Considerations for Switzerland

Healthcare is excellent but expensive: A simple emergency room visit can cost hundreds of Swiss francs. Travel insurance prevents unexpected out-of-pocket expenses.

Mountain Rescue Insurance: Switzerland is mountainous—if you're engaging in outdoor sports, make sure your plan includes *airlift or mountain rescue*. Some policies include this, others require an add-on.

ETIAS Travel Authorization: Once ETIAS goes live, proof of valid travel insurance may be part of the application process for certain travelers.

4. Recommended Providers

Look for well-known international insurers such as:

Allianz Travel

World Nomads

AXA Assistance

SafetyWing (for long stays or digital nomads)

Always compare plans on an aggregator like **Squaremouth**, **InsureMyTrip**, or **VisitorsCoverage**, ensuring you read the fine print.

Final Tips:

Keep **printed and digital copies** of your insurance policy with you.

Know how to **file a claim**—some insurers have apps or toll-free support.

If engaging in winter sports or alpine travel, confirm that **off-piste skiing or high-altitude trekking** is included.

Swiss Pass & Other Transport Cards

Switzerland is renowned for its world-class, efficient, and scenic public transportation system. For travelers, the **Swiss Travel Pass** and other regional passes offer excellent value and flexibility.

1. Swiss Travel Pass (2025 Edition)

This is the most popular transport pass for tourists visiting Switzerland. It allows **unlimited travel** on the Swiss public transportation network.

Key Features:

Unlimited travel by train, bus, and boat across the entire country

Access to premium scenic routes (e.g., Glacier Express, Bernina Express—reservation fees may apply)

Free or discounted entry to over **500 museums**

Free travel on **public transport in more than 90 towns and cities**

Available for **3, 4, 6, 8, or 15 consecutive days**

Best For: Tourists planning to visit multiple cities or take scenic train rides.

2. Swiss Half Fare Card

This card allows travelers to purchase tickets for trains, buses, boats, and most mountain railways at **50% off**.

Key Features:

Valid for one month

Great for travelers staying longer or not traveling every day

Can be combined with individual point-to-point tickets or regional passes

Best For: Visitors who want flexibility and plan to travel at a slower pace.

3. Regional Travel Passes

Perfect for those staying in one area. Options include:

Berner Oberland Regional Pass: Covers Interlaken, Grindelwald, Lauterbrunnen, and surrounding mountain transport.

Tell-Pass (Central Switzerland): Covers Lucerne, Mt. Pilatus, Mt. Titlis, and boat cruises on Lake Lucerne.

Jungfrau Travel Pass: Covers most of the Jungfrau region (Interlaken to Jungfraujoch).

Ticino Ticket: Offers free or reduced public transport in the Ticino (southern) region—often included with hotel stays.

Pro Tips:

Use the **SBB Mobile App** to check train times, buy tickets, and use your pass digitally.

Scenic trains often require **seat reservations** even with a pass.

Children under 6 travel free; those under 16 travel free with the **Swiss Family Card** (available free with the Swiss Travel Pass).

Chapter 2: Getting to Switzerland

Major International Airports in Switzerland

Switzerland has a well-connected network of international airports that make arriving from around the world easy and convenient. Here are the three primary entry points:

1. Zurich Airport (ZRH) – Zurich

Switzerland's largest and busiest airport

Located about 13 km (8 miles) north of Zurich city center

Excellent connections to **Europe, North America, Middle East, and Asia**

Integrated with the **Swiss Rail system**—trains depart directly from the airport station

Services include luggage delivery to hotels, day rooms, and multilingual staff

Best For: Travelers heading to Zurich, Lucerne, Bern, and eastern Switzerland.

2. Geneva Airport (GVA) – Geneva

Located near the French-Swiss border; about 5 km (3 miles) from Geneva city center

Serves major European cities, the Middle East, and some transatlantic flights

Connected to the train network; free transport tickets available in the baggage claim area for visitors staying in Geneva

Best For: Access to Geneva, Lausanne, Montreux, and the French Alps.

3. EuroAirport Basel-Mulhouse-Freiburg (BSL/MLH/EAP)

Unique tri-national airport operated jointly by Switzerland, France, and Germany

Located near Basel, with access to Switzerland, Alsace (France), and Baden-Württemberg (Germany)

Mainly serves European destinations with budget and regional airlines

Divided into Swiss and French sectors—passengers must choose the correct customs exit

Best For: Access to Basel, Bern, and northwestern Switzerland.

Other Entry Points

Bern Airport: Small airport with limited regional service.

Lugano Airport: Closed to commercial flights; served by Milan airports.

Milan Malpensa Airport (MXP): Popular for accessing **Ticino** and the **Italian-speaking part of Switzerland**—connected by train to Lugano and Bellinzona.

Travel Tip:

Upon landing, it's easy to start exploring right away. Swiss airports are seamlessly integrated into the **Swiss Federal Railway system (SBB)**, making your onward journey efficient and scenic.

Direct Flights from Key Global Cities

Switzerland's main airports—**Zurich (ZRH), Geneva (GVA), and Basel (BSL)**—are well-connected with direct flights from major cities across the globe. In 2025, increased demand for European travel has led to more frequent and convenient flight schedules.

1. From North America

New York (JFK/EWR) → Zurich, Geneva (Daily nonstop by SWISS, United, Delta)

Chicago (ORD) → Zurich (SWISS, United)

Los Angeles (LAX) → Zurich (SWISS, Edelweiss Air)

San Francisco (SFO) → Zurich (SWISS, United)

Toronto (YYZ) → Zurich, Geneva (Air Canada, SWISS)

2. From Europe

London (LHR, LGW, STN) → Zurich, Geneva, Basel (BA, SWISS, easyJet, Ryanair)

Paris (CDG/ORY) → Zurich, Geneva (Air France, SWISS)

Frankfurt (FRA) → Zurich, Geneva, Basel (Lufthansa, SWISS)

Amsterdam (AMS) → All major Swiss airports

Barcelona, Rome, Vienna, Brussels → Regular direct flights available

3. From Asia

Singapore (SIN) → Zurich (SWISS, Singapore Airlines)

Tokyo (NRT/HND) → Zurich (SWISS, ANA)

Delhi & Mumbai → Zurich (SWISS, Air India)

Beijing & Shanghai → Zurich (seasonal, SWISS or codeshare options)

Dubai & Doha → All major airports via Emirates, Qatar Airways, and Etihad

4. From the Middle East & Africa

Dubai (DXB) → Zurich, Geneva (Emirates)

Doha (DOH) → Zurich, Geneva (Qatar Airways)

Tel Aviv (TLV) → Zurich, Geneva (El Al, SWISS)

Johannesburg (JNB) → Zurich (via Middle East or European hubs)

5. From Oceania & South America

No direct flights, but smooth one-stop connections via **Dubai, Doha, Frankfurt, or Amsterdam**.

Pro Tip: Zurich Airport tends to offer the most extensive intercontinental connections, while Geneva serves Western Europe and international organizations.

Train Travel from Neighboring Countries

Switzerland shares borders with **France, Germany, Italy, Austria, and Liechtenstein**—all of which are connected by fast, efficient international train services. The Swiss Federal Railways (SBB) collaborates with neighboring rail companies for smooth cross-border journeys.

1. From France

TGV Lyria high-speed trains link:

Paris to Geneva (3h 5m)

Paris to Lausanne (3h 40m)

Paris to Zurich (4h)

TGV trains are comfortable, fast, and often cheaper when booked early.

2. From Germany

ICE and EuroCity (EC) trains serve:

Frankfurt to Zurich (4h)

Munich to Zurich (4h)

Stuttgart to Zurich (3h)

Hamburg to Basel (6–7h)

Trains run multiple times daily and offer scenic routes.

3. From Italy

EuroCity trains connect:

Milan to Zurich (3h 30m via Gotthard Base Tunnel)

Milan to Lugano/Bellinzona (1h 30m–2h)

Venice to Geneva/Basel (via Milan, change required)

Reservations are often required, especially for Milan-Zurich.

4. From Austria

Direct trains from **Innsbruck and Vienna** to Zurich and St. Gallen.

Vienna to Zurich (8h, daily Railjet trains)

5. From Liechtenstein

Regional trains from **Feldkirch (Austria)** or **Buchs SG (Switzerland)** allow easy access to Liechtenstein.

Border & Ticket Tips:

All train routes into Switzerland are **Schengen Zone** routes—no border checks, but carry your passport.

Use the **Eurail or Interrail Global Pass** if traveling to multiple countries, or buy point-to-point tickets via **SBB.ch** or **trainline.eu**.

Trains are punctual, clean, and often faster than short-haul flights when considering airport transfer time.

Would you like sample itineraries combining flights and scenic train routes?

Customs & Immigration Tips

Switzerland, while not a member of the EU, is part of the **Schengen Area**. This means that passport control and customs procedures are streamlined, but there are still specific entry and exit rules to follow.

1. Passport & Visa Control

Schengen Visa Holders: If you have a valid Schengen visa or are from a visa-exempt country (e.g., USA, Canada, UK, Australia, most EU countries), you can enter Switzerland without additional documentation.

Passport Validity: Ensure your passport is **valid for at least 3 months beyond your planned departure** from the Schengen zone and was **issued within the last 10 years**.

Border Checks: While internal Schengen borders are open, random checks can occur. Always carry your passport or national ID.

2. ETIAS (Starting mid-2025)

ETIAS (European Travel Information and Authorization System) will be required for visa-exempt travelers.

It's **not a visa**, but a mandatory pre-travel authorization.

You'll need to apply online, pay a small fee, and receive approval before departure.

Applies to citizens of countries like the U.S., Canada, Australia, etc.

Check etias.europa.eu for current launch updates.

3. Customs Allowances

Duty-Free Limits:

Tobacco: 200 cigarettes or 50 cigars or 250g of tobacco

Alcohol: 1 liter of spirits (>18% alcohol) or 2 liters of wine

Gifts & Goods: Up to **CHF 300** per person without customs declaration

Food & Animal Products: Restricted – avoid bringing meat, dairy, or large amounts of food without checking Swiss import regulations.

4. Currency Declarations

You may carry any amount of cash, but amounts **exceeding CHF 10,000** must be declared to customs.

Always retain receipts when entering with high-value items (e.g., cameras, electronics) to avoid taxation confusion on departure.

5. Green & Red Channels

Use the **Green Channel** if you have nothing to declare.

Use the **Red Channel** if you exceed allowances or carry dutiable goods.

Switzerland Travel Guide 2025`

Chapter 3: Getting Around Switzerland

Swiss Rail Network Overview

Switzerland boasts one of the most **efficient, scenic, and comprehensive** railway networks in the world, operated primarily by the **Swiss Federal Railways (SBB/CFF/FFS)**.

1. Key Features

Punctuality: Swiss trains are famous for being on time—delays over 5 minutes are rare.

Coverage: The network covers nearly all cities, towns, and many rural villages. Even remote alpine areas are accessible by train.

Frequency: Major routes run every 30 minutes or hourly.

Scenic Views: Even regular commuter lines offer stunning lake and mountain scenery.

2. Major Train Types

InterCity (IC): Connects major cities like Zurich, Geneva, Lucerne, Basel, Bern, and Lausanne.

InterRegio (IR): Slightly slower than IC, serving regional hubs.

RegioExpress (RE) & Regional Trains (R): Local trains that connect smaller towns and villages.

S-Bahn Networks: City commuter rail systems in Zurich, Bern, Geneva, Basel, and others.

3. Scenic Train Routes (Book in Advance)

Glacier Express: Zermatt to St. Moritz – dubbed the "slowest express train in the world."

Bernina Express: Chur to Tirano (Italy) – spectacular alpine and glacial scenery.

GoldenPass Line: Lucerne to Montreux – beautiful lakes and mountain vistas.

Gotthard Panorama Express: Combines train and boat across central Switzerland.

4. Ticketing & Travel Passes

Swiss Travel Pass: Unlimited access to trains, buses, boats, and museums.

Point-to-point tickets: Buy individually through SBB.ch or the SBB Mobile App.

Saver Day Pass: Great deal if bought early—valid for unlimited travel on a chosen day.

Seat Reservations: Usually not required except for scenic trains.

5. Connections & Integration

Trains are seamlessly integrated with **buses, ferries, and cable cars**.

Timetables are synchronized, minimizing wait times.

Most stations offer amenities like baggage lockers, cafés, and free Wi-Fi.

Pro Travel Tips:

Use the **SBB Mobile App** for schedules, real-time updates, and digital ticketing.

Most stations have **English-speaking staff** and multilingual signage.

Consider **luggage forwarding services** for ease of travel, especially if heading to mountain resorts.

Driving in Switzerland

Driving in Switzerland can be an unforgettable experience—offering flexibility and access to alpine villages, scenic mountain passes, and off-the-beaten-path destinations. However, it also comes with strict rules, high standards, and well-maintained infrastructure.

1. Driver's License Requirements

Tourists can drive with a **valid foreign driver's license** for up to **one year**.

If your license is **not in English, German, French, or Italian**, an **International Driving Permit (IDP)** is recommended.

2. Road Conditions

Roads are **exceptionally well-maintained**, even in mountainous areas.

Signage is clear, multilingual (often with icons), and speed limits are well-marked.

3. Swiss Motorway Vignette (Toll Sticker)

To drive on highways, you **must purchase a vignette** (CHF 40 for the calendar year).

It's available at gas stations, border crossings, and online.

From 2025, **digital vignettes** are also valid—linked to your license plate.

4. Speed Limits

Urban areas: **50 km/h**

Rural roads: **80 km/h**

Highways: **120 km/h**

Strict enforcement with speed cameras—fines are high and non-negotiable.

5. Parking

Limited and expensive in cities.

Use blue zones (with a parking disc) or white-marked paid spots.

Avoid yellow zones—they're reserved.

Many towns offer **park-and-ride (P+R)** facilities.

6. Mountain Roads

Narrow and winding—drive cautiously.

In winter, **snow tires** are mandatory, and **chains may be required**.

Passes like **Furka, Grimsel, and Susten** offer stunning views but are often **closed in winter**.

7. Fuel & Electric Vehicles

Fuel is readily available; stations are self-service and accept cards.

Switzerland supports electric vehicles with a growing network of **EV charging stations**—especially along highways and in cities.

8. Car Rental Tips

Major rental companies: Europcar, Hertz, Sixt, Avis.

4WD or snow-equipped vehicles are wise in winter.

Cross-border travel is usually allowed but check policies and fees.

Public Transportation in Cities

Swiss cities boast some of the **most efficient, clean, and timely** public transportation systems in the world. Urban travel is smooth, safe, and environmentally friendly.

1. Modes of Transport

Trams: Backbone of city transit in Zurich, Basel, Bern, and Geneva. Fast and frequent.

Buses: Serve areas not covered by trams; well-integrated into the network.

S-Bahn/Regional Trains: Ideal for suburban and cross-city travel (e.g., Zurich S-Bahn).

Trolleybuses: Electrified buses in some cities (e.g., Lucerne).

Boats/Ferries: Operate on lakes in Zurich, Geneva, Lucerne, and others—scenic and functional.

2. Tickets and Passes

One ticket covers multiple modes (tram, bus, local train) within a fare zone.

Buy at stations, vending machines, or via mobile apps (SBB, ZVV, or local transport apps).

Swiss Half Fare Card or **Swiss Travel Pass** often includes urban transport.

Most cities offer **24-hour or multi-day passes**—cheaper and more convenient than single fares.

3. Frequency and Timeliness

Daytime frequency: every 5–10 minutes on main lines.

Nighttime service: Limited, but major cities have **night buses/trams on weekends**.

Always on time—delays are rare and communicated instantly via apps.

4. Accessibility

Wheelchair-friendly trams and buses.

Real-time route info and stop announcements help travelers with disabilities or language barriers.

5. Safety & Cleanliness

Public transport is extremely safe, even at night.

Vehicles are clean and well-maintained, with courteous passengers.

6. City-Specific Highlights

Zurich: Largest and most extensive tram network in the country.

Geneva: Strong bus and tram system; Lake Geneva ferries are part of the transport network.

Basel: Cross-border trams serve parts of Germany and France.

Lucerne: Compact but efficient trolleybus and boat network.

Insider Tip: For tourists staying in hotels in cities like Geneva, Lucerne, Bern, and Lausanne, **free public transport cards** are often provided for the duration of your stay.

Scenic Train Journeys (Glacier Express, Bernina Express, etc.)

Switzerland's scenic train rides are legendary, offering panoramic views of mountains, lakes, glaciers, and charming alpine villages—all from the comfort of a carriage. These routes are more than transportation—they're unforgettable experiences.

1. Glacier Express

Route: Zermatt to St. Moritz (or reverse)

Duration: ~8 hours

Highlights: Matterhorn views, Landwasser Viaduct, Rhine Gorge (Swiss Grand Canyon), Oberalp Pass

Features: Panoramic windows, 3-course meals, luxury Excellence Class (with personal concierge)

Booking Tip: Seat reservations are **mandatory** and should be made well in advance—especially in summer and winter.

2. Bernina Express

Route: Chur / St. Moritz to Tirano (Italy)

Duration: ~4 hours

Highlights: UNESCO World Heritage Albula & Bernina Lines, Lago Bianco, Morteratsch Glacier, Brusio Spiral Viaduct

Features: Panoramic coaches, multilingual audio guides, and breathtaking photo stops

Bonus: Connects to the **Bernina Express Bus** from Tirano to Lugano through Italy and southern Switzerland.

3. GoldenPass Line

Route: Lucerne – Interlaken – Zweisimmen – Montreux

Duration: ~5.5 hours (can be done in segments)

Highlights: Lake Lucerne, the Bernese Oberland, scenic vineyards of Montreux, and alpine villages

Unique Option: The GoldenPass Express offers direct connections without changing trains between Interlaken and Montreux.

4. Gotthard Panorama Express

Route: Lucerne to Lugano (via boat and train)

Duration: ~5.5 hours

Highlights: Lake Lucerne boat cruise, historic Gotthard route, spiral tunnels, Ticino's Mediterranean flair

Experience: Combines ferry and panoramic train for a varied journey.

5. Voralpen-Express

Route: Lucerne to St. Gallen

Duration: ~2.5 hours

Highlights: Gentle pre-Alpine scenery, Lake Zurich, rolling hills and meadows

Good For: Less touristy, ideal for relaxing travel between central and eastern Switzerland.

Bike Rentals and Walking Trails

Switzerland is a dream for active travelers. With extensive bike routes and world-class walking trails, it's easy to explore the landscape at your own pace.

Bike Rentals

Where to Rent:

Most cities and towns offer rentals through shops, train stations, or digital platforms like **Rent a Bike**, **Publibike**, and **Donkey Republic**.

E-bikes are widely available, ideal for hilly terrain.

Pricing: Starts at CHF 15–25/day for regular bikes and CHF 30–50/day for e-bikes.

One-Way Rentals: Available via major rail stations—pick up in one city and drop off in another.

Bike Transport on Trains: Bikes are allowed on most trains with a **bike day pass** (~CHF 14) or with a reservation on busy routes.

Popular Cycling Routes

Lake Geneva Loop: Gentle, scenic, and perfect for wine and lake views.

Rhine Route (EuroVelo 15): Runs from Andermatt to Basel—suitable for all fitness levels.

Lakes Trail: Combines several small lakes and quiet forest paths in central Switzerland.

Jura Bike Trail: More demanding route across the Jura Mountains—great for MTB and e-bike enthusiasts.

Walking Trails

Switzerland maintains over **65,000 km** of marked hiking and walking trails, categorized for different skill levels:

Urban & Easy Walks

Zurich's Lake Promenade: A leisurely walk along Lake Zurich with cafés and parks.

Geneva to Carouge: Combines city charm and local markets with riverside paths.

Lucerne City Walks: Wooden Chapel Bridge, Old Town, and lakeside strolls.

Scenic & Thematic Walks

Five Lakes Walk (Zermatt): Iconic reflections of the Matterhorn in alpine lakes.

Lavaux Vineyard Terraces (UNESCO site): Trails with views of Lake Geneva and centuries-old vineyards.

Eiger Trail: High-Alpine trail near Grindelwald, beneath the north face of the Eiger.

Mountain & Nature Walks

Oeschinensee Panorama Trail (Kandersteg): Leads to one of Switzerland's most beautiful mountain lakes.

Aletsch Glacier Trail: Views of the longest glacier in the Alps.

Creux du Van (Neuchâtel Jura): Dramatic limestone cliffs and wildlife.

Pro Tips:

Signage: Yellow signs = walking trails; red & white = mountain hikes; blue & white = alpine/mountaineering paths.

Maps & Apps: Use **SwitzerlandMobility**, **AllTrails**, or **SBB Mobile** for route planning and trail info.

Safety: Always check the weather, wear good footwear, and bring water—especially in alpine areas.

Would you like a suggested 3- or 5-day itinerary that combines scenic trains and outdoor adventures?

Switzerland Travel Guide 2025`

Chapter 4: Where to Stay in Switzerland

Top Cities and Regions for Accommodation

1. Zurich – Cosmopolitan Comfort and Convenience

Best for: First-time visitors, business travelers, nightlife seekers

Switzerland's largest city offers a wide variety of accommodations—from sleek boutique hotels in the Old Town to business-friendly stays near the airport or central station.

Highlights: Proximity to Lake Zurich, world-class museums, restaurants, Bahnhofstrasse shopping, and excellent transport links.

Recommended Areas: Altstadt (Old Town), Enge (lake access), and Zürich West (trendy and modern).

2. Lucerne – Scenic Beauty and Historic Charm

Best for: Romantic getaways, culture lovers, easy access to the Alps

A storybook city with a medieval old town, lakeside promenades, and mountain views.

Highlights: Close to Mt. Pilatus and Mt. Rigi, the Chapel Bridge, and lake cruises.

Recommended Areas: Old Town for charm, Tribschen for quiet stays near the lake.

3. Geneva – International and Elegant

Best for: Diplomats, luxury travelers, cultural explorers

Known for its upscale hotels, global cuisine, and lakefront beauty, Geneva is ideal for travelers who enjoy cosmopolitan vibes with a French twist.

Highlights: United Nations HQ, Jet d'Eau, art galleries, and proximity to the French Alps.

Recommended Areas: Paquis (lakefront), Old Town, and Eaux-Vives (vibrant local life).

Switzerland Travel Guide 2025`

4. Interlaken – Adventure Base in the Bernese Oberland

Best for: Outdoor adventurers, nature lovers, thrill seekers

A perfect base for exploring the Jungfrau Region, Interlaken is nestled between Lake Thun and Lake Brienz.

Highlights: Paragliding, canyoning, hiking, day trips to Lauterbrunnen, Grindelwald, and Jungfraujoch.

Recommended Areas: Interlaken West for budget travelers; Interlaken Ost for quick train access to mountain resorts.

5. Zermatt – Alpine Luxury at the Foot of the Matterhorn

Best for: Skiers, hikers, and mountain lovers

A car-free village renowned for winter sports and luxury lodges.

Highlights: Views of the Matterhorn, Gornergrat Railway, skiing, and gourmet dining.

Recommended Areas: Central Zermatt (close to lifts and restaurants); outskirts for quieter luxury chalets.

6. Bern – Switzerland's Underrated Capital

Best for: History buffs, families, relaxed city breaks

A UNESCO World Heritage Site with cobblestone streets, arcades, and bear pits.

Highlights: Federal Palace, Einstein Museum, and riverside walks.

Recommended Areas: Old Town (Altstadt), Breitenrain (residential and quiet), and Kirchenfeld (near museums).

7. Lausanne – Youthful Energy on Lake Geneva

Best for: Students, solo travelers, lake lovers

A hilly city with a vibrant arts scene, world-class sports facilities (Olympic Museum), and easy lake access.

Highlights: Lavaux vineyards, Lausanne Cathedral, Ouchy waterfront.

Recommended Areas: Flon (trendy), Ouchy (by the lake), and Old Town.

8. Lugano – Swiss-Mediterranean Flair

Best for: Romantic escapes, foodies, warm-weather travelers

Italian-speaking and palm-lined, Lugano blends Swiss precision with Italian passion.

Highlights: Monte Brè, Parco Ciani, lakeside cafes, and nearby Italian border towns.

Recommended Areas: City center, lakeside promenade, or nearby villages like Gandria for serenity.

9. Basel – Art, Architecture & Tri-Border Access

Best for: Art lovers, business travelers, cultural tourists

With 40+ museums, this city straddles Germany and France.

Highlights: Art Basel, Fondation Beyeler, Rhine cruises.

Recommended Areas: Old Town (Altstadt), Kleinbasel (younger crowd), and near the Messe (trade fair area).

10. The Bernese Oberland – Quintessential Switzerland

Best for: Classic alpine scenery, rail journeys, peace and quiet

Base yourself in villages like **Lauterbrunnen**, **Wengen**, **Grindelwald**, or **Mürren** for jaw-dropping views and access to some of Switzerland's most iconic hikes and trains.

Luxury Hotels & Resorts

Switzerland is home to some of the most luxurious hotels in the world, offering an unparalleled experience for travelers seeking comfort and elegance. From stunning alpine resorts to historic city hotels, these accommodations provide exceptional service, breathtaking views, and world-class amenities, making them the perfect choice for a memorable Swiss vacation.

1. **Badrutt's Palace Hotel, St. Moritz**

Badrutt's Palace Hotel is a landmark in St. Moritz, renowned for its blend of classic charm and modern sophistication. The hotel has been synonymous with luxury for over a century, offering guests exceptional service and stunning views of the Swiss Alps.

Location:

Address: Via Serlas 27, 7500 St. Moritz, Switzerland

Proximity: Situated in the heart of St. Moritz, it's within walking distance of the ski slopes and the famous St. Moritz lake.

Highlights:

Panoramic views of the surrounding mountains.

Historical ambiance with modern luxury.

Private ski lifts and direct access to the slopes in winter.

Spa and Wellness:

The Palace Spa features treatments inspired by Swiss alpine nature.

A state-of-the-art fitness center, saunas, and an outdoor heated pool are available for relaxation.

Bars:

The King's Club, one of the most exclusive nightclubs in Switzerland.

The elegant Chesa Veglia, a historic former farmhouse, offers a cozy yet upscale atmosphere.

Events and Conferences:

A vast selection of meeting rooms for conferences, with full business services.

The hotel has hosted numerous high-profile events and private gatherings.

Basic Facilities and Amenities:

24-hour concierge, valet service, and transportation.

Luxury boutiques, ski storage, and an art gallery.

Ski equipment rentals and personalized ski services.

Opening and Closing Hours:

Open year-round.

The restaurants, bars, and spa operate from 10:00 AM to midnight (hours may vary seasonally).

Price:

Room rates start at around CHF 1,200 per night, with luxury suites going up to CHF 10,000 per night depending on the season.

Pros:

Unmatched luxury and top-notch service.

Exclusive access to ski slopes.

Ideal for both winter sports enthusiasts and those looking for a tranquil getaway.

Cons:

Extremely high price point.

The location may feel remote for guests seeking easy access to city life.

Local Tips:

If visiting during ski season, book ski lessons and equipment rentals in advance, as they tend to get booked quickly.

Don't miss out on dinner at Chesa Veglia, where the atmosphere is unique and the food is exceptional.

2. The Dolder Grand, Zurich

The Dolder Grand is one of Zurich's most prestigious hotels, offering a fusion of luxury, style, and comfort. It's perched high above the city, offering sweeping views of Lake Zurich, the Alps, and the surrounding cityscape.

Location:

Address: Kurhausstrasse 65, 8032 Zurich, Switzerland

Proximity: Just a 15-minute drive from Zurich's city center and the main train station.

Highlights:

The hotel's architecture blends traditional and contemporary design.

The impressive art collection featuring works by Picasso and other famous artists.

Spa and Wellness:

The Dolder Grand Spa is one of the largest and most luxurious in Europe, offering everything from thermal baths to massages and exclusive beauty treatments.

Bars:

The stylish "The Lounge" serves a wide range of cocktails with beautiful views.

The "Cigar Lounge" offers a relaxing environment for cigar lovers.

Events and Conferences:

With over 20 meeting rooms and ballrooms, The Dolder Grand caters to high-profile corporate events and private celebrations.

Offers customized event planning services for conferences and weddings.

Basic Facilities and Amenities:

Helicopter pad, private parking, and valet services.

Multiple dining options, including Michelin-starred restaurants.

Concierge service, luxury shopping boutiques, and extensive meeting facilities.

Opening and Closing Hours:

Open year-round.

Spa hours: 9:00 AM to 9:00 PM.

Restaurant and bars typically open from 12:00 PM to 10:00 PM.

Price:

Rooms start at CHF 800 per night, with suites ranging up to CHF 5,000 per night.

Pros:

Stunning views and elegant design.

Award-winning spa and wellness facilities.

Excellent for both business and leisure travelers.

Cons:

High-end luxury comes with a hefty price tag.

Can feel somewhat isolated from the city's main attractions.

Local Tips:

Take a stroll in the nearby Dolderwald forest to enjoy panoramic views of Zurich.

Book dinner at the restaurant "The Restaurant" to experience fine dining with a Michelin star.

3. **Kulm Hotel, St. Moritz**

Kulm Hotel is a historic gem in the heart of St. Moritz, renowned for its unrivaled luxury and spectacular views. It's a perfect destination for those who want to enjoy a refined Swiss vacation with access to skiing, gourmet dining, and top-tier services.

Location:

Address: Via Veglia 18, 7500 St. Moritz, Switzerland

Proximity: Conveniently located near the St. Moritz train station and just a short walk from the ski slopes.

Highlights:

A prime location offering views of Lake St. Moritz and the surrounding mountains.

A rich history, dating back to 1856, and a heritage of luxury service.

Spa and Wellness:

The Kulm Spa offers an extensive range of wellness treatments, including massages, facials, and a variety of saunas.

A fitness center and an indoor pool complement the wellness offerings.

Bars:

The Kulm Bar is a popular spot for après-ski drinks and offers a wide selection of wines and cocktails.

Events and Conferences:

The hotel offers multiple event spaces, including a grand ballroom and meeting rooms, suitable for corporate events, weddings, and other celebrations.

Basic Facilities and Amenities:

24-hour concierge, ski butlers, and a ski shuttle service.

Fine dining restaurants, a wine cellar, and luxury boutiques.

Opening and Closing Hours:

Open year-round.

Spa facilities open from 10:00 AM to 8:00 PM.

Price:

Rates begin at CHF 900 per night, with deluxe suites priced upwards of CHF 6,000 per night during peak seasons.

Pros:

Ideal for those seeking both luxury and outdoor activities.

A mix of modern comforts with historical charm.

Exceptional service and personalized experiences.

Cons:

Pricing is on the high side.

Can be quite busy during ski season.

Local Tips:

Visit the nearby St. Moritz lake for a picturesque winter setting.

Consider booking a private ski instructor to enhance your skiing experience.

4. Badrutt's Palace Hotel, Gstaad

A world-class luxury hotel, the Badrutt's Palace in Gstaad offers a serene mountain retreat with unmatched elegance. It has been serving the elite for decades, offering a blend of sophisticated style and first-class amenities.

Location:

Address: Badrutt's Palace Hotel, CH-3780 Gstaad, Switzerland

Proximity: Gstaad village center is just a few minutes away by car.

Highlights:

The stunning alpine setting, perfect for skiing, hiking, and mountain biking.

Exclusive private villas and suites offering an elevated level of luxury.

Spa and Wellness:

Features a modern spa with rejuvenating treatments, saunas, and an indoor pool.

Full-service beauty treatments available.

Bars:

Enjoy cocktails at the chic Palace Bar, overlooking the Swiss Alps.

Events and Conferences:

The hotel offers several event spaces that cater to large conferences, private meetings, and weddings.

Basic Facilities and Amenities:

Ski-in, ski-out access, luxury shopping, and a full-service concierge.

Gourmet restaurants, wine cellar, and a piano bar.

Opening and Closing Hours:

Year-round operation.

The spa and wellness center operates from 9:00 AM to 8:00 PM.

Price:

Nightly rates start from CHF 1,000, with suites and luxury villas costing much more.

Pros:

Perfect for those who enjoy skiing and mountain activities.

Top-tier amenities and facilities, including a ski school and wellness center.

Cons:

Very expensive, especially during the winter season.

Remote location may not appeal to those seeking city life.

Local Tips:

Explore the nearby Saanenland region for scenic hikes and Swiss alpine villages.

Gstaad has a luxury shopping scene—don't miss a visit to the local boutiques.

5. Badrutt's Palace Hotel, Lucerne

OThis iconic hotel combines the best of Swiss elegance and high-end luxury, with breathtaking views of Lake Lucerne and the Alps. It offers a quiet escape with easy access to the cultural and historical attractions of Lucerne.

Location:

Address: Badrutt's Palace Hotel, Lucerne, Switzerland

Proximity: Situated along Lake Lucerne, it's a short walk from the city's historical district and attractions.

Highlights:

Beautiful lakeside views and historical charm.

Luxury amenities including private suites with panoramic vistas.

Spa and Wellness:

Offers a full-service wellness center with relaxing treatments, a sauna, and a fitness center.

Bars:

The lobby bar offers classic cocktails, ideal for a relaxing evening by the lake.

Events and Conferences:

Multiple event rooms suitable for small meetings or larger conferences.

Basic Facilities and Amenities:

On-site fine dining restaurants, valet parking, and concierge services.

Luxury boutiques and wellness options.

Opening and Closing Hours:

Open year-round.

Restaurants, bars, and spa facilities operate from 9:00 AM to 10:00 PM.

Price:

Rates begin at CHF 950 per night, with suites and luxury rooms reaching upwards of CHF 5,000 per night.

Pros:

Convenient location for tourists interested in Lucerne's cultural scene.

Gorgeous lake views and luxurious amenities.

Cons:

The price point is very high.

The hotel's popularity means it's often fully booked during peak seasons.

Local Tips:

Take a boat ride across Lake Lucerne to experience the stunning Swiss landscape.

Visit the nearby Mount Pilatus for hiking or a cable car ride to the summit.

Mid-Range Options

For those seeking comfort and quality at a more affordable price, Switzerland offers a variety of mid-range hotels. These accommodations provide excellent service, stylish rooms, and convenient locations, allowing visitors to enjoy a comfortable stay without breaking the bank. Whether nestled in charming towns or near popular attractions, mid-range options are ideal for tourists looking to balance luxury and value.

1. Hotel des Balances, Lucerne

Located in the heart of Lucerne, Hotel des Balances offers a historic yet modern experience. With its beautiful lakeside views and central location, it provides guests with easy access to the city's main attractions while maintaining a charming, traditional Swiss atmosphere.

Location:

Address: Weinmarkt, 6004 Lucerne, Switzerland

Proximity: Situated in the town center, just a few steps from the Chapel Bridge, the Old Town, and the lake.

Highlights:

Views of Lake Lucerne and the Swiss Alps.

Close to cultural landmarks, shopping, and dining.

Spa and Wellness:

The hotel doesn't have a full spa but offers wellness services including a sauna and fitness center.

Bars:

The hotel features a lakeside terrace and a cocktail bar with stunning views of the water.

Events and Conferences:

Several meeting and conference rooms equipped with modern technology.

Switzerland Travel Guide 2025`

Basic Facilities and Amenities:

Free Wi-Fi, air conditioning, and a 24-hour front desk.

Restaurant offering Swiss cuisine and international dishes.

Opening and Closing Hours:

Open year-round.

The restaurant serves meals from 7:00 AM to 10:00 PM, while the bar is open in the evenings.

Price:

Rooms start at around CHF 250 per night.

Pros:

Central location in Lucerne with easy access to the city's highlights.

Beautiful lakeside views at an affordable price.

Cons:

Can be crowded, especially during peak tourist seasons.

Rooms can be on the smaller side compared to more expensive luxury hotels.

Local Tips:

Visit the nearby Richard Wagner Museum for a cultural experience.

Consider taking a boat tour on Lake Lucerne to enjoy the scenic beauty.

2. Hotel Waldhaus, Sils-Maria

Hotel Waldhaus is a charming, family-owned hotel located in the picturesque village of Sils-Maria in the Swiss Alps. This hotel blends tradition with modern amenities, offering a peaceful retreat ideal for those who enjoy nature and outdoor activities.

Location:

Address: Sils-Maria, 7514 Engadine, Switzerland

Proximity: Situated in a tranquil area near hiking and skiing trails, and just a short drive from St. Moritz.

Highlights:

Ideal for nature lovers with extensive hiking and skiing options.

A historic hotel with a rich cultural heritage.

Spa and Wellness:

The hotel offers a wellness center with a sauna, a steam bath, and massage services.

Bars:

The hotel features a cozy bar with a great selection of wines and local spirits.

Events and Conferences:

Small conference rooms suitable for meetings, along with catering services for events.

Basic Facilities and Amenities:

Free Wi-Fi, private parking, and ski storage.

On-site restaurant serving Swiss and Mediterranean cuisine.

Opening and Closing Hours:

Open year-round.

The wellness area operates from 9:00 AM to 7:00 PM.

Price:

Rooms start at CHF 200 per night.

Pros:

Located in a scenic and quiet area, perfect for relaxation and outdoor activities.

Family-friendly atmosphere with a traditional touch.

Cons:

Remote location may not be convenient for tourists seeking proximity to cities.

Smaller compared to larger hotels, with limited amenities.

Local Tips:

Explore the nearby Fex Valley for stunning Alpine scenery.

In winter, take advantage of the nearby cross-country skiing trails.

3. Hotel Arosa, Zermatt

Hotel Arosa in Zermatt provides a cozy, modern retreat in one of Switzerland's top ski resorts. Known for its excellent service, the hotel offers a perfect mix of modern comfort and alpine charm, ideal for skiers, nature lovers, and those seeking a laid-back mountain experience.

Location:

Address: Seilerwiesen, 3920 Zermatt, Switzerland

Proximity: Close to Zermatt's railway station and within easy access to ski lifts, hiking trails, and the iconic Matterhorn Glacier.

Highlights:

Gorgeous views of the Matterhorn Mountain.

Traditional Alpine architecture with modern comfort.

Spa and Wellness:

The hotel features a spa and wellness center with an indoor pool, sauna, and massage services.

Bars:

A lounge bar with an extensive list of cocktails, local wines, and spirits.

Events and Conferences:

The hotel offers small event spaces for meetings, with services tailored to corporate or social gatherings.

Switzerland Travel Guide 2025`

Basic Facilities and Amenities:

Free Wi-Fi, ski storage, and a shuttle service to ski lifts.

On-site restaurant offering Swiss specialties and international cuisine.

Opening and Closing Hours:

Open year-round.

The spa and wellness area operates from 10:00 AM to 7:00 PM.

Price:

Rooms start at around CHF 300 per night.

Pros:

Located in one of Switzerland's top ski resorts, ideal for winter sports enthusiasts.

Great views of the Matterhorn.

Cons:

Higher prices during peak ski seasons.

Can be a bit noisy, especially when the hotel is busy with tourists.

Local Tips:

Take a ride on the Gornergrat Railway for a breathtaking panoramic view of the Matterhorn.

During the summer, hike the Zermatt Glacier or explore the region's scenic trails.

4. Hotel Bristol, Geneva

Hotel Bristol is an elegant and well-positioned mid-range hotel in the heart of Geneva. Known for its central location, excellent service, and refined atmosphere, this hotel is perfect for both business travelers and tourists wanting to explore the city's sights.

Location:

Address: 10, rue du Mont-Blanc, 1201 Geneva, Switzerland

Proximity: Just steps from Lake Geneva, the train station, and the city's shopping districts.

Highlights:

Close proximity to key landmarks, including the Jet d'Eau fountain and Parc des Bastions.

Classic Swiss hospitality with modern touches.

Spa and Wellness:

Offers a wellness area with a sauna and massage services.

A small fitness room is also available for guests.

Bars:

The hotel's bar is a great spot for enjoying a drink after a day of sightseeing, with a selection of wines, cocktails, and light bites.

Events and Conferences:

Several meeting rooms are available for small business conferences or events.

Basic Facilities and Amenities:

Free Wi-Fi, air conditioning, and a 24-hour concierge.

On-site restaurant offering Swiss and international dishes.

Opening and Closing Hours:

Open year-round.

The restaurant serves from 7:00 AM to 10:00 PM, and the bar is open in the evenings.

Price:

Rooms start at CHF 220 per night.

Pros:

Ideal for tourists wanting to be close to Geneva's top attractions.

Comfortable rooms with modern amenities.

Cons:

Can be on the expensive side for a mid-range hotel.

Limited amenities compared to larger luxury hotels.

Local Tips:

Take a boat ride on Lake Geneva and explore nearby Mont Blanc.

Visit the United Nations headquarters and the International Red Cross Museum while in Geneva.

5. Hotel Schweizerhof, Bern

Hotel Schweizerhof is located in the historic center of Bern, offering both traditional Swiss hospitality and modern comforts. It's perfect for those looking to explore Bern's cultural landmarks while staying in a comfortable and well-equipped hotel.

Location:

Address: Bahnhofplatz 11, 3011 Bern, Switzerland

Proximity: Located near Bern's train station, with easy access to the Old Town and major cultural attractions.

Highlights:

Historic building with a classic Swiss ambiance.

Close to Bern's UNESCO World Heritage-listed Old Town.

Spa and Wellness:

The hotel offers a wellness area with a sauna and a small fitness center.

Bars:

The hotel's bar serves a variety of cocktails and local beverages.

Events and Conferences:

The hotel provides a variety of meeting spaces with modern technology and full event services.

Basic Facilities and Amenities:

Free Wi-Fi, concierge services, and luxury dining options.

On-site restaurant specializing in Swiss and Mediterranean cuisine.

Opening and Closing Hours:

Open year-round.

Restaurant hours are from 6:30 AM to 10:00 PM, and the bar operates in the evening.

Price:

Rooms start at CHF 250 per night.

Pros:

Excellent location for exploring Bern's Old Town.

A blend of modern amenities with Swiss charm.

Cons:

Rooms can be on the smaller side.

Higher rates during peak tourist seasons.

Local Tips:

Explore Bern's beautiful Old Town, including the Zytglogge clock tower and Bern Cathedral.

Visit the Bear Park for a peaceful walk and to see the city's emblematic bears.

Budget Stays & Hostels

Switzerland also offers budget-friendly stays and hostels for travelers seeking affordable accommodation without compromising on comfort. These options provide basic amenities, clean environments, and a social atmosphere, making them perfect for backpackers or those on a tighter budget. Whether in city centers or scenic areas, budget stays and hostels offer a great way to experience Switzerland without overspending.

1. Youth Hostel Zurich

Youth Hostel Zurich is an excellent option for those looking for affordable accommodation in the city while enjoying clean, modern facilities. Located near the central train station, it's ideal for travelers wishing to explore Zurich without spending too much.

Location:

Address: Mutschellenstrasse 114, 8048 Zurich, Switzerland

Proximity: Only a short distance from Zurich's city center, the main train station, and close to the beautiful Lake Zurich.

Facilities and Amenities:

Offers both shared dormitories and private rooms.

On-site restaurant serving affordable meals.

Free Wi-Fi and communal kitchen facilities.

Laundry services and bike rentals available.

Price:

Dormitory beds start at CHF 40 per night, and private rooms start at CHF 90.

Pros:

Very affordable, especially for budget-conscious travelers.

Central location with easy access to public transport.

Offers a social atmosphere with plenty of common areas for meeting other travelers.

Cons:

Shared facilities like bathrooms and kitchens might not offer the same privacy as more expensive options.

Can be crowded, especially during peak travel seasons.

Local Tip:

Take advantage of the hostel's bicycle rental service to explore Zurich at your own pace, as the city is very bike-friendly.

2. Geneva Hostel, Geneva

Situated on the edge of Lake Geneva, Geneva Hostel is a great option for those looking to stay in Switzerland's second-largest city without breaking the bank. The hostel offers a combination of dormitory-style and private rooms, all with views of the lake or the nearby mountains.

Location:

Address: Quai du Mont-Blanc 26, 1201 Geneva, Switzerland

Proximity: Close to the city's main attractions, including the Jet d'Eau fountain, the Old Town, and the International Red Cross Museum.

Facilities and Amenities:

Free breakfast served daily.

Private rooms with lake views and shared dorms.

A fully-equipped kitchen for self-catering.

Free Wi-Fi, laundry facilities, and a spacious lounge area.

Price:

Dormitory beds start at CHF 35 per night, and private rooms start at CHF 90.

Pros:

Beautiful location by the lake with amazing views.

Good facilities, including a kitchen for cooking your own meals.

Ideal for those on a tight budget who still want to be close to Geneva's attractions.

Cons:

The hostel can get crowded in the high season.

Geneva tends to be more expensive compared to other Swiss cities, so this hostel can still feel pricey for some.

Local Tip:

Take a free public transport pass provided by the hostel to explore Geneva more economically.

3. Backpacker Hostel, Interlaken

Interlaken, known for its stunning Alpine views and adventure sports, is a popular tourist destination. Backpacker Hostel offers affordable dormitory beds and private rooms with an inviting, relaxed atmosphere, ideal for those looking to explore the outdoor activities Interlaken is famous for.

Location:

Address: Höheweg 71, 3800 Interlaken, Switzerland

Proximity: Centrally located, a short walk from the train station and just a short distance from the outdoor adventure hubs, including paragliding and skiing activities.

Facilities and Amenities:

Offers both dormitory and private rooms.

On-site café and bar for budget-friendly meals and drinks.

Free Wi-Fi, a communal kitchen, and laundry facilities.

Outdoor garden space with BBQ facilities.

Price:

Dormitory beds start at CHF 35 per night, and private rooms start at CHF 70.

Pros:

Very affordable for Interlaken, which is often a more expensive destination.

Close to both Interlaken West and Interlaken Ost stations, making it convenient for those traveling by train.

Great place to meet fellow travelers and enjoy the relaxed atmosphere.

Cons:

Shared facilities may not offer the privacy some travelers prefer.

Can be noisy due to its popularity among younger travelers.

Local Tip:

If you're an adventure lover, make sure to book your outdoor activities (like paragliding or hiking) early in the season, as they fill up quickly.

4. Motel des Alpes, Lausanne

Motel des Alpes offers basic yet comfortable accommodation in the vibrant city of Lausanne. Located in a central area, it provides easy access to Lausanne's cultural attractions, the Olympic Museum, and the shores of Lake Geneva.

Location:

Address: Rue de la Barre 1, 1005 Lausanne, Switzerland

Proximity: Just a 10-minute walk from Lausanne's train station, close to local shops, cafes, and museums.

Facilities and Amenities:

Offers simple rooms with private bathrooms.

Free Wi-Fi throughout the property.

A small on-site restaurant serving continental breakfasts.

Accessible public transport options nearby.

Price:

Rooms start at CHF 80 per night.

Pros:

Budget-friendly in an otherwise expensive city like Lausanne.

Great location with easy access to public transport and city attractions.

Private rooms provide more comfort and privacy than typical hostels.

Cons:

Rooms are basic with minimal amenities.

Some rooms may be small compared to more expensive hotels.

Local Tip:

Explore the nearby Lavaux Vineyard Terraces, a UNESCO World Heritage site just a short train ride away from Lausanne.

5. The Matterhorn Hostel, Zermatt

Zermatt, famous for its skiing and views of the Matterhorn, is a popular destination, but it can also be quite expensive. The Matterhorn Hostel offers a budget-friendly option for those who want to visit this iconic location without spending a fortune.

Location:

Address: Vispastrasse 6, 3920 Zermatt, Switzerland

Proximity: Located in the town center, only a few minutes' walk from Zermatt's main train station and close to ski lifts.

Facilities and Amenities:

Offers shared dormitories as well as private rooms.

Free Wi-Fi and a fully-equipped kitchen.

A common area for relaxation and socializing.

Locker facilities and ski storage.

Price:

Dormitory beds start at CHF 35 per night, and private rooms start at CHF 80.

Pros:

Excellent value for money considering Zermatt's high prices.

Convenient location with easy access to ski slopes and hiking trails.

Offers both dorms and private rooms, providing flexibility for different types of travelers.

Cons:

The hostel can get busy, especially in peak seasons.

Shared bathrooms and kitchens may not suit all travelers.

Local Tip:

Take the Gornergrat Railway for a panoramic view of the Matterhorn, or hike the surrounding mountains if you're visiting in summer.

Booking Tips for 2025

When planning a trip to Switzerland in 2025, it's important to consider various factors that will help you secure the best deals, optimize your travel experience, and ensure smooth bookings. Here are some useful booking tips for tourists looking to travel to Switzerland in 2025:

1. Book Early for Peak Seasons

Switzerland's peak tourist seasons, such as summer (June-August) and winter (December-February), attract large numbers of visitors. To get the best prices and availability, it's recommended to book your accommodation, transport, and tours at least 4-6 months in advance, especially if you're planning to visit popular destinations like Zermatt, Interlaken, or Lucerne.

Why it matters:

Booking early gives you access to more options and lower prices.

Popular hotels and attractions can get fully booked quickly, especially during peak times like ski season and summer holidays.

2. Use Price Comparison Websites

For flights and hotels, using price comparison websites can help you find the best deals. Platforms like Skyscanner, Google Flights, Booking.com, and Kayak allow you to compare prices from various providers, ensuring that you get the best value for your money.

Why it matters:

Price comparison tools provide transparency and ensure you're not overpaying for your flight or accommodation.

Alerts for price drops can also help you secure cheaper deals closer to your travel date.

3. Consider Alternative Airports

Switzerland has multiple international airports that are well-connected to major cities. While Zurich and Geneva are the most popular, consider flying into smaller airports like Basel or Bern for potential savings on flights.

Why it matters:

Smaller airports may offer cheaper flights, especially if you're traveling on a budget.

You can easily reach major cities via train or shuttle services, as Switzerland has an excellent public transport network.

4. Take Advantage of Rail Passes

Switzerland has one of the best public transportation systems in the world. If you're planning to explore multiple regions, consider purchasing a **Swiss Travel Pass** or a **Swiss Half Fare Card**. These passes allow unlimited travel on trains, buses, and boats across Switzerland for a set period.

Why it matters:

Rail passes offer savings on transport costs and allow you to travel freely across the country, making it more cost-effective if you plan to visit several cities or regions.

The Swiss Travel Pass also gives you access to discounts on mountain excursions and free entry to many museums.

5. Flexible Travel Dates for Lower Prices

If you have flexibility in your travel dates, consider adjusting your trip slightly to take advantage of lower rates. Travel during the shoulder seasons (May, September, and October) to avoid the crowds and high prices of summer and winter.

Why it matters:

Flights, accommodation, and tours tend to be cheaper during shoulder seasons.

You'll also enjoy fewer crowds and a more relaxed experience at popular tourist spots.

6. Book Directly with Hotels and Providers

After comparing prices on booking websites, consider booking directly with the hotel or tour provider. Many Swiss hotels and operators offer perks or discounts for direct bookings, such as free upgrades, breakfast, or discounts on additional services.

Why it matters:

Direct bookings may come with added benefits that are not available through third-party websites.

Hotels sometimes offer lower rates for direct reservations to avoid commission fees charged by booking platforms.

7. Look for Packages or Group Deals

Many tour operators offer package deals that combine flights, accommodation, and tours. If you're planning to visit multiple Swiss cities or regions, you might find better deals in packages or group tours. It can be especially beneficial for those visiting Switzerland for the first time.

Why it matters:

Package deals can save you money compared to booking everything separately.

Group tours may offer special discounts and include transportation, which is often more convenient and economical than handling each detail on your own.

8. Check for Last-Minute Deals

If you're a flexible traveler with an adventurous spirit, last-minute deals can offer significant savings. Websites like HotelTonight and Lastminute.com list discounts for travelers willing to book their stays at the last moment.

Why it matters:

Hotels and airlines sometimes offer last-minute discounts to fill empty rooms or seats.

It's a great option if you're spontaneous and can adapt to last-minute availability.

9. Review Cancellation Policies

When booking in 2025, ensure you carefully review the cancellation policies for hotels, flights, and tours. Look for flexible or refundable options in case your travel plans change.

Why it matters:

Switzerland is a popular destination, and plans can change unexpectedly, especially with travel restrictions or unforeseen events.

Flexible cancellation policies provide peace of mind, allowing you to change or cancel your booking without losing your money.

10. Be Mindful of Local Holidays and Events

Switzerland has a number of national holidays and regional events, such as the **Montreux Jazz Festival** or **Geneva International Motor Show**, which can cause accommodation prices to rise and attractions to be more crowded. Make sure to research local holidays or events happening during your stay.

Why it matters:

Being aware of special events helps you plan your trip better, as some hotels and activities may require advanced reservations or might be fully booked.

It allows you to avoid busy periods if you prefer a quieter experience.

11. Opt for Local, Authentic Experiences

While booking tours and activities in Switzerland, prioritize local experiences that give you an authentic feel for the country. This could include a scenic boat ride on Lake Lucerne, a hike in the Swiss Alps, or a cheese fondue dinner in a traditional Swiss restaurant.

Why it matters:

Local experiences offer a unique perspective on Swiss culture and are often more affordable than commercialized tours.

Booking local tours directly with the operators can help you avoid higher commission rates charged by third-party booking sites.

Chapter 5: Top Destinations in Switzerland

Zurich: Financial Capital Meets Culture

Zurich is the largest city in Switzerland and serves as the financial capital of the country. It is home to a global financial hub and boasts some of the world's highest living standards. However, Zurich is far from just a business city; it is also an extraordinary cultural and artistic center, offering a fantastic blend of modernity and tradition.

Financial Powerhouse and Global Connectivity

Zurich's financial sector is its backbone, with major banks, investment firms, and multinational corporations headquartered in the city. For those interested in finance or economics, Zurich is an exciting city to explore, with many opportunities to learn about its central role in the global financial system.

The city's Bahnhofstrasse is one of the world's most exclusive shopping streets, lined with luxury boutiques, jewelers, and high-end retailers. The presence of Swiss financial institutions and international firms gives Zurich a cosmopolitan atmosphere, making it a vital player in global commerce.

Cultural Hotspot

Despite its financial prominence, Zurich offers a rich cultural landscape. The city is home to world-class museums, galleries, and theaters. The **Zurich Kunsthaus (Zurich Art Museum)** houses an impressive collection of modern art, showcasing works from masters like Van Gogh, Chagall, and Giacometti. Art lovers will also appreciate the **Museum Rietberg**, dedicated to non-European art, which offers a deep dive into the art and culture of Africa, Asia, and the Americas.

Zurich is also renowned for its vibrant music scene. Whether you are a fan of classical music or contemporary beats, you will find an event or concert to match your taste. The **Zurich Opera House** offers breathtaking performances, while the **Kaufleuten** is a popular venue for modern music, attracting top artists from around the globe.

The Charm of the Old Town (Altstadt)

Zurich's Old Town, or Altstadt, is a captivating area that transports visitors back in time. Cobblestone streets, medieval buildings, and narrow alleys form a picturesque setting. The **Grossmünster Church**, one of Zurich's most iconic landmarks, offers a chance to explore Swiss Reformation history, while the **Fraumünster Church** is famous for its beautiful stained-glass windows designed by Marc Chagall.

The vibrant atmosphere of Altstadt is complemented by trendy cafes, boutique shops, and fine restaurants. Enjoy a leisurely stroll along the **Limmat River**, or take a boat ride on Lake Zurich to experience the beauty of the city from a different perspective.

Nature and Outdoor Activities

Zurich's location at the foot of the Alps means that outdoor activities are never far away. In the winter, Zurich becomes a haven for ski enthusiasts, and in the summer, the surrounding mountains and lakes offer the perfect setting for hiking, swimming, and sailing. Zurich's proximity to nature allows visitors to balance the busy urban experience with peaceful moments by the lake or in the mountains.

Geneva: International Flavor by the Lake

Geneva, known for its multinational organizations and stunning lakeside setting, is another of Switzerland's top destinations. As the headquarters of major international organizations, including the United Nations and the Red Cross, Geneva is often referred to as the "Peace Capital" of the world. The city's unique position at the border of France and Switzerland also gives it a blend of French and Swiss cultures, which enhances its global appeal.

A Global Hub for Diplomacy

Geneva has long been recognized for its role as a hub for international diplomacy and humanitarian efforts. The presence of the **United Nations Office at Geneva** and the **World Health Organization** makes it one of the most important centers for international governance and global policy discussions. The **Palais des Nations**, located on the banks of Lake Geneva, is a fascinating site to visit. Guided tours offer visitors the opportunity to see where key decisions affecting global peace, security, and development are made.

Moreover, the **International Red Cross and Red Crescent Museum** offers a moving and informative experience about the organization's efforts in global humanitarian aid, providing insight into its historic role and current operations.

Breathtaking Lake Geneva and Surroundings

One of Geneva's most striking features is its location on the shores of Lake Geneva, one of the largest lakes in Europe. The lake's crystal-clear waters, surrounded by the Alps, create a picturesque landscape that is hard to match. Visitors can enjoy scenic boat cruises, offering stunning views of the city and the surrounding mountains. Along the lakeside, the **Jet d'Eau**, a towering water fountain, is a notable symbol of Geneva, shooting water 140 meters into the air.

Geneva's lakefront is lined with beautiful parks, such as the **English Garden**, where visitors can stroll through manicured lawns, see sculptures, or relax by the water. The city's proximity to the Alps and surrounding vineyards offers numerous opportunities for hiking, wine tasting, and exploring quaint villages like **Montreux** and **Vevey**, both easily accessible from Geneva.

Cultural Heritage and Events

Like Zurich, Geneva is home to a variety of cultural attractions. The **Museum of Art and History** showcases Geneva's artistic legacy, while the **Musée d'ethnographie** offers fascinating insights into the world's diverse cultures. In addition, the city is known for hosting major events such as the **Geneva International Film Festival** and the **Fête de l'Escalade**, a historic celebration of the city's victory over the Duke of Savoy's forces in 1602.

The city's rich multiculturalism is reflected in its culinary scene. From French-inspired haute cuisine to international fare, Geneva's food offerings cater to all tastes. The city is particularly renowned for its fondue, chocolate, and wine – all of which are highlights of any trip to Switzerland.

The Old Town (Vieille Ville)

Geneva's Old Town is another must-see area. It's a charming, historical neighborhood with cobblestone streets and quaint buildings. Here, you'll find the **St. Pierre Cathedral**, which offers panoramic views of the city from its tower, and the **Maison Tavel**, a museum that traces Geneva's history from Roman times to the present day.

Lucerne: Medieval Charm and Lake Views

Lucerne, nestled between the shores of Lake Lucerne and the towering Swiss Alps, is one of the most picturesque cities in Switzerland. With its medieval charm, historical significance, and stunning natural surroundings, Lucerne is a must-visit destination for tourists who appreciate history, culture, and breathtaking views.

Historical Significance

Lucerne's history dates back to the Middle Ages, and it retains much of its medieval charm. The **Chapel Bridge (Kapellbrücke)**, a covered wooden bridge built in the 14th century, is one of Lucerne's most iconic landmarks. It is decorated with beautiful 17th-century paintings that depict the city's history and are displayed under the bridge's roof. The **Water Tower**, which stands next to the Chapel Bridge, is also a significant historical feature of the city.

The **Old Town (Altstadt)** of Lucerne is a captivating area with cobbled streets, colorful buildings, and picturesque squares. Walking through this area feels like stepping back in time, as the medieval architecture is remarkably well-preserved. The **Musegg Wall**, a 14th-century fortification, offers another glimpse into Lucerne's past and provides panoramic views of the city.

Stunning Lake Lucerne

Lake Lucerne is renowned for its pristine beauty, and the surrounding mountains provide a dramatic backdrop. The lake is often referred to as one of the most beautiful lakes in Europe. Visitors can take a boat cruise across the lake, which allows for stunning views of the surrounding landscape, including the snow-capped peaks of Mount Pilatus and Mount Rigi.

For those seeking a closer connection to nature, a visit to **Mount Pilatus** or **Mount Rigi** is highly recommended. Both mountains are accessible via cable cars and cogwheel trains and offer stunning views of the Swiss Alps, Lake Lucerne, and the surrounding countryside. The area is perfect for hiking, skiing, and other outdoor activities.

Cultural Attractions

Lucerne also boasts a vibrant cultural scene. The **Swiss Museum of Transport** is one of the country's most visited museums, offering interactive exhibits on

Switzerland's transportation history, including trains, automobiles, and airplanes. The **Richard Wagner Museum**, dedicated to the famous composer who lived in the area, is another cultural highlight.

The **Lucerne Festival** is an annual classical music event that attracts top musicians and orchestras from around the world. The **Culture and Congress Centre (KKL)**, designed by architect Jean Nouvel, is a modern architectural gem and hosts a wide range of cultural events throughout the year, from concerts to theater performances.

The Lion Monument

A touching tribute to the Swiss Guards who were killed during the French Revolution, the **Lion Monument** is one of Lucerne's most moving landmarks. The monument, carved into a sandstone rock face, depicts a lion mourning the loss of its comrades. It's a symbol of loyalty and sacrifice and is a must-see for visitors interested in Swiss history.

Bern: UNESCO-listed Capital

Bern, the capital of Switzerland, is a charming city that combines history, culture, and stunning natural beauty. The city's Old Town, which is a UNESCO World Heritage site, is a highlight, featuring well-preserved medieval architecture and scenic views of the Aare River. With its picturesque streets, historical buildings, and a welcoming atmosphere, Bern offers visitors a glimpse into Switzerland's rich history and cultural heritage.

UNESCO World Heritage Old Town

The historic Old Town of Bern is one of the most beautiful in Switzerland, with its narrow, cobbled streets, ancient fountains, and medieval buildings. The **Zytglogge (Clock Tower)**, a 13th-century tower with an astronomical clock, is one of the city's most recognizable landmarks. Every hour, the clock chimes, and visitors gather to watch the mechanical figures perform a fascinating show.

The **Bern Cathedral (Münster)**, Switzerland's tallest cathedral, is another notable attraction in the Old Town. Climbing the tower offers a stunning panoramic view of the city, the Aare River, and the surrounding mountains.

Cultural Heritage

Bern is rich in cultural attractions, and the **Bern Historical Museum** is one of the most significant. The museum offers an in-depth look at Swiss history, including exhibits on the country's art, archaeology, and cultural heritage. The **Einstein Museum**, located in the house where Albert Einstein lived while working at the Swiss Patent Office, explores the life and work of this groundbreaking physicist.

Another key cultural attraction in Bern is the **Rosengarten (Rose Garden)**, which provides breathtaking views of the city and the Alps in the distance. The garden is home to over 200 varieties of roses and is the perfect spot for a peaceful stroll or a picnic.

The Aare River and Surrounding Views

The Aare River winds through the heart of Bern, and the city's location along the river provides spectacular views of the surrounding landscape. Visitors can take a leisurely walk along the riverbanks or enjoy a boat tour. The **Gurten Hill**, located just outside the city, offers panoramic views of Bern and the surrounding countryside and is a great place for hiking or a scenic train ride.

Bern is also known for its traditional markets, especially the **Zibelemärit (Onion Market)**, held annually in November. The market is a celebration of the region's agricultural traditions and includes an array of local products, from onions to cheeses and meats, as well as arts and crafts.

Bear Park and the Symbol of Bern

One of the city's most unique features is the **Bear Park**, which is located near the Old Town. The park is home to a number of brown bears, which are the symbol of Bern. The bears have lived in the city for centuries, and today, visitors can see them in a natural habitat setting along the banks of the Aare River.

Lausanne: Culture & Vineyards

Located on the shores of Lake Geneva, **Lausanne** is a city known for its sophisticated cultural scene, its proximity to wine-producing regions, and its stunning views of the surrounding Alps. As the fourth-largest city in Switzerland, Lausanne seamlessly blends modernity with tradition, offering an exceptional combination of art, history, and natural beauty.

Cultural Heritage and Museums

Lausanne is a cultural powerhouse, home to a variety of world-class museums, galleries, and theaters. The **Olympic Museum**, located in Lausanne, is one of the city's most prominent attractions. The city is home to the **International Olympic Committee**, and the museum offers a fascinating look at the history of the Olympic Games, showcasing memorabilia, interactive exhibits, and the spirit of international sportsmanship.

Another key cultural institution in Lausanne is the **Musée de l'Elysée**, dedicated to the art of photography. This museum is internationally recognized and offers a chance to explore the history and evolution of photography through carefully curated exhibitions.

For lovers of contemporary art, the **Collection de l'Art Brut** showcases works by self-taught artists, many of whom are outsiders in the traditional art world. These galleries offer a unique insight into raw, creative expressions that stand apart from mainstream art movements.

The Old Town (Vieille Ville)

Lausanne's **Old Town** is a delightful maze of medieval streets, steep inclines, and historical landmarks. The **Lausanne Cathedral (Cathédrale de Notre-Dame)** is one of Switzerland's finest Gothic structures and offers stunning views of the city from its tower. Visitors can explore the impressive interior, which includes beautifully stained-glass windows, and admire the stunning architecture of this iconic building.

The **Place de la Palud** is a charming square in the heart of the Old Town, where visitors can experience the city's historic vibe and enjoy a coffee at one of the local cafés while watching the famous animated clock show. Lausanne's cobbled streets and narrow alleys make it a perfect place to explore on foot, with each turn offering something new, from historical buildings to quaint shops and restaurants.

Vineyards and Lake Geneva

One of Lausanne's most distinctive features is its location within the **Lavaux Vineyards**, a UNESCO World Heritage site. The terraced vineyards that stretch along the shores of Lake Geneva offer stunning views of the lake, the surrounding Alps, and the meticulously maintained rows of grapevines. Visitors can explore the vineyards through walking or biking tours, enjoying the scenic beauty while learning about the wine-making process. The region is known for its **Chasselas** wine, and there are numerous local wineries where tourists can taste the wines and purchase bottles to take home.

A boat ride on **Lake Geneva** is another way to enjoy the beauty of Lausanne. The city's lakeside is lined with parks and promenades, providing a peaceful setting to relax and take in the scenery. Whether you're enjoying a glass of local wine on a boat or relaxing by the lake at sunset, the views are spectacular and make Lausanne a perfect destination for nature lovers and wine enthusiasts alike.

Events and Festivals

Lausanne is also known for hosting a range of cultural events throughout the year. The **Festival de la Cité** is an annual cultural festival that celebrates music, theater, dance, and visual arts, attracting international artists. The **Lausanne Underground Film & Music Festival (LUFF)** is another significant event, highlighting avant-garde films and music from around the world. These festivals add to the city's vibrant atmosphere, making it an exciting place to visit for those who love culture and the arts.

Basel: Art, Architecture & Rhine River

Basel is Switzerland's third-largest city and is often considered the country's cultural capital. Situated on the banks of the **Rhine River**, Basel offers an incredible mix of art, architecture, history, and a lively atmosphere. Known for its unique blend of old and new, Basel is a city where tradition meets modernity in the fields of art, design, and architecture.

Art and Museums

Basel is internationally renowned for its vibrant art scene. The city is home to some of the most important art institutions in Europe, including the **Kunstmuseum Basel**, which houses an outstanding collection of artworks from the Middle Ages to the present day. Visitors can view works by artists such as **Van Gogh**, **Picasso**, and **Holbein**, as well as contemporary art pieces that reflect the cutting edge of the art world.

Art Basel, the world-famous contemporary art fair, is held annually in the city and attracts artists, collectors, and art lovers from across the globe. It is a major event in the international art calendar, showcasing the work of emerging artists as well as established figures in the contemporary art world.

The **Vitra Design Museum**, located just outside Basel, is another must-visit for design enthusiasts. It offers a deep dive into architecture and design, featuring both permanent and temporary exhibits on the evolution of design and iconic architects.

Architecture

Basel is a haven for architecture lovers. The city is home to a diverse range of architectural styles, from medieval buildings to modern masterpieces. The **Basel Minster**, a stunning Gothic cathedral that dates back to the 12th century, dominates the skyline and offers breathtaking views over the Rhine River and the city. Visitors can explore its grand architecture, intricate stained-glass windows, and peaceful surroundings.

In contrast, the modern architecture of **Fondation Beyeler**, designed by architect Renzo Piano, highlights the city's commitment to contemporary design. The museum's sleek, modern lines blend harmoniously with its natural surroundings, offering an experience that pairs art with architecture.

Another architectural highlight is the **Kunsthalle Basel**, an important venue for contemporary art exhibitions, housed in a beautiful 19th-century building. Basel's architectural diversity makes it an exciting destination for anyone interested in design and urban development.

The Rhine River

The **Rhine River** is a central feature of Basel, and a walk along its banks offers stunning views of the city and surrounding areas. The **Mittlere Brücke** (Middle Bridge), dating back to the 13th century, is the city's oldest bridge and a great spot to take in views of the river. Visitors can enjoy boat cruises along the Rhine, which offer a unique perspective of the city and its landmarks.

One of Basel's most popular summer traditions is the **Basler Fasnacht**, a lively, colorful carnival held annually in February or March. The event, which celebrates the city's rich traditions, features parades, elaborate costumes, and street performances. It's an experience that highlights Basel's vibrant local culture.

Food and Drink

Basel is also known for its culinary delights. The city offers a variety of fine dining options, as well as traditional Swiss and regional dishes. Local specialties include **Basler Läckerli** (a type of honey and almond biscuit) and **Älplermagronen** (a Swiss pasta dish). The city's proximity to both French and German borders influences its cuisine, resulting in a mix of flavors that appeal to food lovers.

Interlaken: Gateway to the Alps

Nestled between **Lake Thun** and **Lake Brienz** in the heart of the Bernese Oberland region, **Interlaken** is often referred to as the "Gateway to the Alps." With its stunning mountain views and a wide range of adventure activities, it is a paradise for nature lovers and thrill-seekers alike.

Adventure Capital

Interlaken has earned its reputation as Switzerland's adventure capital, attracting outdoor enthusiasts from around the world. The surrounding mountains, including the **Eiger**, **Mönch**, and **Jungfrau**, provide a stunning backdrop for an array of activities such as **paragliding, skydiving, bungee jumping**, and **canyoning**. Paragliding from the nearby **Harder Kulm** offers a spectacular bird's-eye view of the town and surrounding lakes, while the thrill of tandem skydiving allows visitors to leap from an aircraft with a view of the snow-capped Alps.

Interlaken is also a popular base for those looking to explore the Jungfrau region, including the famous **Jungfraujoch**, the highest railway station in Europe. A cogwheel train journey takes you up to the "Top of Europe," where you can enjoy panoramic views of glaciers and snow-covered peaks, visit the Ice Palace, and take part in snow activities.

Scenic Beauty and Outdoor Activities

In addition to adrenaline-pumping activities, Interlaken offers plenty of opportunities for more serene outdoor experiences. The nearby lakes, **Lake Thun** and **Lake Brienz**, offer peaceful boat cruises with stunning views of the mountains. The **Schilthorn** and **Harder Kulm** provide easy access to viewpoints with panoramic vistas of the Swiss Alps. The area also features an extensive network of hiking and biking trails that offer opportunities to explore the beautiful alpine landscape at a more leisurely pace.

Cultural and Historical Attractions

While Interlaken is best known for outdoor adventures, it also offers cultural and historical sites. The **Hohematte Park**, located in the heart of the town, is a lovely place to relax and enjoy the view of the mountains. The **Interlaken Monastery** and **Trummelbach Falls**, a series of stunning waterfalls inside a mountain, are also popular attractions. Additionally, Interlaken's historic buildings, such as the **Casino Interlaken**, give the town a charming blend of the past and present.

Jungfrau Region

Interlaken serves as a gateway to the **Jungfrau Region**, which includes some of Switzerland's most iconic destinations, such as **Grindelwald**, **Lauterbrunnen**, and **Wengen**. These picturesque mountain villages offer easy access to hiking, skiing, and glacier excursions, making them popular with tourists year-round. The Jungfrau Region is also known for the **Eiger Trail**, which is a world-renowned hiking route that leads along the base of the Eiger Mountain.

Zermatt: Home of the Matterhorn

Zermatt is one of the most famous mountain resorts in Switzerland, and its main claim to fame is its proximity to the **Matterhorn**, one of the most iconic peaks in the world. This small, car-free village at the foot of the Matterhorn offers stunning views, exceptional skiing, and an authentic alpine experience.

The Matterhorn

The **Matterhorn** is undoubtedly one of the most photographed mountains in the world. Its pyramid-like shape makes it instantly recognizable, and Zermatt offers the perfect base for visitors wishing to admire this majestic peak. Whether from the village itself, on a hike, or while skiing, the Matterhorn is always within view, offering a mesmerizing experience for those lucky enough to see it up close.

For those who are keen to explore the Matterhorn, the **Matterhorn Glacier Paradise** is an extraordinary experience. Accessible via the highest cable car station in Europe, visitors can get panoramic views of the Matterhorn and surrounding peaks, explore ice caves, and even try skiing or snowboarding on glaciers in the summer.

Skiing and Winter Sports

Zermatt is renowned for its exceptional skiing and winter sports. The resort offers some of the best skiing conditions in Switzerland, with a massive interconnected ski area that spans both Switzerland and Italy, known as the **Matterhorn Glacier Ski Paradise**. Zermatt boasts over 360 kilometers of pistes, making it a haven for skiers and snowboarders of all levels. Visitors can also enjoy snowshoeing, tobogganing, and ice climbing in the winter months.

Zermatt is famous for its long ski season, which extends from late November to May, thanks to its high altitude and glacier skiing opportunities. In addition to skiing, visitors can enjoy scenic cable car rides, snowboarding, and even a range of après-ski options, from cozy mountain huts to lively bars and restaurants.

Hiking and Mountaineering

In addition to winter sports, Zermatt is a prime location for hiking and mountaineering in the summer. There are countless trails that offer jaw-dropping views of the surrounding mountains and glaciers. The **Gornergrat** railway, which ascends to a breathtaking viewpoint with a view of the Matterhorn, is a popular way to experience the surrounding beauty.

For more serious mountaineers, Zermatt is a launching point for some of the most famous climbs in the Alps, including expeditions to the Matterhorn itself. The village has a rich mountaineering history, and the **Matterhorn Museum** is an excellent place to learn about the history of the region and the challenges of climbing the iconic peak.

Car-Free Village and Alpine Charm

One of Zermatt's most unique features is that it is a car-free village, which preserves the peaceful, alpine charm of the region. Visitors travel by electric taxis, horse-drawn carriages, or simply on foot, making for a tranquil atmosphere with no vehicle noise. The pedestrian streets are lined with shops, restaurants, and luxury hotels, many of which offer stunning views of the Matterhorn.

The village's alpine charm is complemented by a range of excellent dining options, including Swiss specialties like fondue, raclette, and local Valais wines. Zermatt offers an unparalleled combination of adventure, relaxation, and breathtaking natural beauty.

Gorner Glacier and Theodul Pass

Beyond the Matterhorn, Zermatt is home to the **Gorner Glacier**, one of the largest glaciers in the Alps. The glacier is accessible by a scenic train ride or hike and offers a chance to explore its ice caves and crevasses. Another notable attraction is the **Theodul Pass**, which forms the historic border between Switzerland and Italy and was once a major route for traders.

Lugano: Swiss-Mediterranean Charm

Located in the southern part of Switzerland, **Lugano** offers visitors a unique blend of Swiss efficiency and Mediterranean charm. Situated in the Italian-speaking region of Ticino, Lugano is blessed with a mild climate, stunning lake views, and an atmosphere that feels more Mediterranean than Swiss. With its picturesque lakeside setting and the majestic backdrop of the Alps, Lugano is a destination for both relaxation and cultural exploration.

Lakeside Beauty and Outdoor Activities

Lugano is beautifully positioned along **Lake Lugano**, which is surrounded by hills and mountains, creating a stunning natural setting. The lake offers opportunities for sailing, swimming, and boat tours, providing panoramic views of the city and the surrounding landscape. The **Parco Ciani**, a lakeside park with beautiful trees and benches, is a lovely place for a leisurely walk or a picnic with a view.

For those who enjoy outdoor adventures, **Monte Brè** and **Monte San Salvatore** offer hiking trails, funicular rides, and incredible views of both the lake and the Alps. The cable car ride up Monte San Salvatore is especially popular, offering visitors sweeping views of Lugano and the surrounding region. Hiking and mountain biking are also popular activities here, with trails suitable for all levels of outdoor enthusiasts.

Mediterranean Influence and Culture

Lugano's Mediterranean influence is evident in its cuisine, architecture, and lifestyle. The city boasts a range of Italian-inspired restaurants, cafes, and gelaterias. Dining in Lugano often includes local specialties like risotto, polenta, and fresh fish from the lake, along with fine Italian wines. This southern influence gives the city an inviting, relaxed atmosphere, in contrast to the more traditional Swiss cities in the country's northern regions.

The architecture of Lugano also reflects its Italian influence, with elegant villas and buildings showcasing Mediterranean designs, often surrounded by lush gardens and palm trees. The **Lugano Art and Culture Center (LAC)** is an excellent place to explore the city's cultural side, hosting a variety of performances, from opera to contemporary art exhibitions. **Villa Favorita**, a historic villa turned museum, offers insight into the region's art and history, while the **Museo d'Arte della Svizzera italiana** showcases Swiss and Italian artworks from the Renaissance to the modern day.

Charming Old Town

Lugano's **Old Town (Centro Storico)** is a charming mix of narrow streets, colorful buildings, and open squares, ideal for strolling and exploring. **Piazza della Riforma** is the heart of the Old Town, where you'll find vibrant cafes and shops with a distinctly Mediterranean flair. The **Lugano Cathedral** (Cattedrale di San Lorenzo) is another historical landmark in the Old Town, offering sweeping views of the surrounding area from its bell tower.

One of the unique features of Lugano is its proximity to Italy. Just a short drive away, visitors can cross the border and enjoy the Italian culture, food, and shopping in nearby towns like **Mendrisio** or **Como**. This close connection to Italy enriches the experience for those traveling to Lugano, offering a taste of both Swiss and Italian lifestyles.

Year-Round Events and Festivals

Lugano is also known for its lively cultural scene. The **Lugano Festival**, held annually, celebrates classical music and attracts world-class performers. The **Moon & Stars** music festival, held every summer, is a popular event featuring international pop and rock artists performing in a beautiful open-air setting. Additionally, the **Lugano Film Festival** celebrates international cinema, further solidifying the city's status as a cultural hotspot.

Switzerland Travel Guide 2025`

Chapter 6: Top Attraction in Switzerland

The Matterhorn

The Matterhorn is one of the most iconic and recognizable mountains in the world, located in the Swiss Alps. Its distinct pyramid-shaped peak is often seen as a symbol of Switzerland itself. It stands at 4,478 meters (14,692 feet) and is one of the highest peaks in Europe. The Matterhorn is a major draw for tourists, mountaineers, and photographers, offering a variety of experiences from skiing to hiking and sightseeing.

Location:
The Matterhorn lies on the border between Switzerland and Italy, specifically between the canton of Valais in Switzerland and the Aosta Valley in Italy. It is located near the town of Zermatt, Switzerland, and can be accessed via various modes of transportation, including trains, cable cars, and hiking trails.

Switzerland Travel Guide 2025`

History:

The Matterhorn has a storied history, particularly in the world of mountaineering. First climbed in 1865 by a British team led by Edward Whymper, the mountain's ascent ended in tragedy as four of the team members fell to their deaths while descending. This tragic event marked the Matterhorn as one of the most challenging mountains to climb. It continues to attract mountaineers, though the mountain is considered highly dangerous, even for experienced climbers.

Opening and Closing Hours:

The Matterhorn itself is a natural landmark and does not have opening or closing hours. However, the facilities around it, such as the Gornergrat Railway and cable cars, do have operating hours. The Gornergrat Railway, for example, operates year-round, typically from early morning until late afternoon, with extended hours in peak seasons.

Top Things to Do:

Gornergrat Railway Ride:

Take the cogwheel train from Zermatt to the Gornergrat, where you'll be treated to stunning views of the Matterhorn and surrounding peaks. It's a great way to see the mountain without having to hike.

Hiking and Mountaineering:

There are numerous hiking trails around the Matterhorn, offering spectacular views of the mountain and the Swiss Alps. One popular route is the Matterhorn Glacier Trail, which takes you up close to glaciers and offers impressive views of the Matterhorn.

Skiing and Snowboarding:

Zermatt is a renowned ski resort, and while the Matterhorn itself is often too treacherous for beginner skiers, its surrounding slopes offer fantastic skiing and snowboarding experiences.

Photography:
The Matterhorn's unique shape makes it a favorite subject for photographers, especially during sunrise and sunset. The reflection of the mountain in nearby lakes, such as the Stellisee, adds to its allure.

Visit the Matterhorn Museum:

Located in Zermatt, the museum showcases the history of the mountain, including its first ascent and the tragedy of 1865. It's a great place to learn more about the mountain's history and its significance to mountaineering.

Tips for Visiting:

Prepare for Altitude: The Matterhorn is high in the Swiss Alps, so visitors should be aware of the potential effects of altitude, such as shortness of breath. Make sure to hydrate and take things slow if you're hiking.

Weather Can Be Unpredictable: Even in the summer months, the weather can change rapidly. Dress in layers and be prepared for cold temperatures, especially at higher elevations.

Advance Booking for Skiing and Tours: If you plan to ski or take a guided tour, booking in advance is highly recommended, especially during peak seasons.

Lake Geneva

Lake Geneva, also known as Lac Léman, is one of Europe's largest lakes, located along the border between Switzerland and France. Known for its stunning scenery, vineyards, and charming lakeside towns, it is a top destination for tourists seeking relaxation, outdoor activities, and cultural experiences. The lake spans an area of 580 square kilometers (224 square miles) and is surrounded by the Alps and Jura mountains, providing breathtaking views from every corner.

Location:
Lake Geneva stretches across the Swiss regions of Vaud, Valais, and Geneva, and it also borders the French department of Haute-Savoie. The city of Geneva lies at the western tip of the lake, while the famous town of Montreux is located along its northern shore. The lake is easily accessible by train, boat, or car from major Swiss cities like Zurich, Lausanne, and Geneva.

History:
Lake Geneva has a rich history, dating back to Roman times, and has been a crossroads for trade and culture for centuries. It has been an important center for industry, arts, and diplomacy. The city of Geneva, which sits at the western

tip of the lake, became a hub for international diplomacy in the 19th and 20th centuries, housing the headquarters of the League of Nations and later, the United Nations Office at Geneva. The lake itself has been central to both local life and the economic development of the region.

Opening and Closing Hours:

Lake Geneva itself is a natural feature and doesn't have set hours. However, many attractions along the lake, including boat tours, museums, and parks, have their own hours of operation. For example, the boat services operate daily during the tourist season, usually from spring to autumn, from morning until evening.

Top Things to Do:

Boat Tours:

A boat tour on Lake Geneva is one of the best ways to enjoy the lake's beauty. You can take scenic cruises between towns like Montreux, Lausanne, and Geneva, each offering stunning views of the Alps and Jura mountains. There are also options for private boat rentals for a more intimate experience.

Visit the Château de Chillon:

Located on the eastern shore of Lake Geneva near Montreux, Château de Chillon is one of Switzerland's most famous historical sites. This medieval castle is perched on a small island and offers a fascinating look into the region's history and architecture. The views from the castle's ramparts over the lake are unparalleled.

Explore the Vineyards of Lavaux:

The Lavaux vineyards, a UNESCO World Heritage site, are located along the northern shore of Lake Geneva, between Lausanne and Montreux. Visitors can stroll through terraced vineyards and sample wines produced from the region's grape varieties, which have been cultivated for centuries.

Geneva's Promenade and Parks:

The city of Geneva offers scenic lakeside promenades and lush parks. The Parc des Bastions and the English Garden are perfect spots for a leisurely stroll or a picnic with views of the lake and the mountains beyond. Don't miss the famous Jet d'Eau, a large fountain that shoots water 140 meters into the air.

Water Sports and Swimming:

Lake Geneva's clean waters and numerous beaches make it an excellent place for swimming, sailing, paddleboarding, and other water sports. During summer, many towns around the lake have public beaches where visitors can enjoy the sun.

Cultural Attractions:

The cities and towns around Lake Geneva offer rich cultural experiences, including art galleries, museums, and theaters. In Geneva, you can visit the Museum of Art and History, while Montreux hosts the famous Montreux Jazz Festival every summer.

Tips for Visiting:

Dress for the Weather: The climate around Lake Geneva can be mild, but the weather can change quickly, especially near the mountains. Bring a jacket and layers, especially in the evening.

Use Public Transport: The public transport system around the lake is efficient, with trains, boats, and buses connecting most major cities and towns. Consider purchasing a Swiss Travel Pass to access these services.

Book in Advance for Festivals: If you're planning to attend events like the Montreux Jazz Festival, it's best to book accommodations and tickets well in advance, as the area gets very busy during peak festival times.

The Jungfrau Region

The Jungfrau Region is one of the most breathtaking areas in the Swiss Alps, known for its majestic peaks, charming villages, and outdoor activities year-round. It includes the famous trio of mountains—Eiger, Mönch, and Jungfrau—and is a haven for hikers, skiers, and sightseers alike. The area's stunning landscapes attract nature lovers, while its well-developed infrastructure makes it accessible to all types of travelers.

Location:
Located in the Bernese Oberland in central Switzerland, the Jungfrau Region includes popular towns such as Grindelwald, Lauterbrunnen, Wengen, and Mürren. The main transportation hub is Interlaken, from where visitors take trains or cable cars into the higher mountain areas.

History:
The Jungfrau was first climbed in 1811, and the region has since become a symbol of Alpine exploration. The construction of the Jungfrau Railway in the early 20th century was a major engineering feat, culminating in the Jungfraujoch station—Europe's highest railway station. Tourism in the region has evolved from elite adventure travel to a popular destination for families and outdoor enthusiasts.

Opening and Closing Hours:

The Jungfrau Region is open year-round. The **Jungfraujoch Railway** typically runs from early morning (around 7:00 AM) to late afternoon (around 4:30–5:00 PM), depending on the season. Cable cars and other transport services have similar schedules.

Top Things to Do:

Visit Jungfraujoch – Top of Europe:

Ride the cogwheel train to the highest railway station in Europe at 3,454 meters. Visit the Ice Palace, Sphinx Observatory, and enjoy panoramic views of the Aletsch Glacier.

Hiking and Scenic Trails:

Trails like the Eiger Trail, Schynige Platte to Faulhorn, and hikes through Lauterbrunnen Valley are among the most scenic in the world.

Winter Sports:

The Jungfrau Region offers world-class skiing and snowboarding, especially around Grindelwald and Wengen.

Explore Alpine Villages:

Visit car-free Mürren or Wengen, traditional villages with charming chalets, stunning views, and relaxed atmospheres.

Tips for Visiting:

Book train tickets to Jungfraujoch early, especially in summer.

Bring layers; temperatures at the top can be freezing even in summer.

Stay at least two days to fully explore the area's highlights.

Château de Chillon

Château de Chillon is Switzerland's most visited historic monument. Perched on a rock along Lake Geneva, this medieval castle combines natural beauty with cultural heritage. With its towers, ramparts, halls, and dungeons, the castle is a window into Switzerland's feudal and literary past.

Location:
Located in Veytaux, near Montreux on the eastern shore of Lake Geneva, the château is easily accessible by train, boat, or car.

History:
The castle dates back to at least the 12th century and was occupied by the Counts of Savoy. It later served as a prison and military post. The famous poet Lord Byron wrote *The Prisoner of Chillon* after visiting the site in 1816, further immortalizing its legend.

Opening and Closing Hours:

Switzerland Travel Guide 2025`

Open Daily: 10:00 AM – 6:00 PM (April to October)

Winter Hours: 10:00 AM – 5:00 PM (November to March)

Last entry is typically one hour before closing.

Closed on December 25 and January 1.

Top Things to Do:

Castle Tour:

Explore 25+ rooms including the Grand Halls, Gothic bedrooms, and the medieval chapel. English audioguides or guided tours are available.

Visit the Dungeon:

Walk through the eerie underground prison where François Bonivard was imprisoned, inspiring Byron's poem.

Lakeside Walks:

Combine your visit with a walk or bike ride along the lakeside promenade between Montreux and Chillon.

Photography:

The castle is one of the most photogenic landmarks in Europe, especially during sunset with the lake and Alps as a backdrop.

Tips for Visiting:

Buy tickets online to skip the line.

Allocate 1.5 to 2 hours for the full visit.

The castle is stroller and wheelchair accessible on the ground floor, but not all levels are accessible.

Interlaken

Interlaken is a resort town nestled between Lake Thun and Lake Brienz, and surrounded by the Bernese Alps. It's a hub for adventure tourism and the gateway to the Jungfrau Region. With its dramatic alpine views, charming streets, and adrenaline activities, Interlaken is ideal for thrill-seekers and nature lovers.

Location:
Located in the Bernese Oberland of central Switzerland, Interlaken sits on the flat area between two lakes and is easily reachable by train from major cities like Zurich, Lucerne, and Bern.

History:
Originally a monastery settlement in the 12th century, Interlaken developed into a tourist destination in the 19th century as visitors flocked to the Alps. It became especially popular with British tourists and remains one of Switzerland's top holiday destinations.

Opening and Closing Hours:

Interlaken, as a town, is always accessible. Tourist attractions, shops, and tour services generally operate from 9:00 AM to 6:00 PM, though adventure tour companies often start early and run activities throughout the day.

Top Things to Do:

Harder Kulm Viewpoint:

Take the funicular up to Harder Kulm for panoramic views of Interlaken, Eiger, Mönch, and Jungfrau.

Adventure Sports:

Interlaken is known as the adventure capital of Switzerland. Try paragliding, skydiving, bungee jumping, or canyoning.

Boat Cruises on Lakes Thun and Brienz:

Enjoy scenic cruises on turquoise lakes surrounded by mountains and waterfalls.

Explore Höhematte Park:

Located in the town center, this park offers great views and is a popular landing area for paragliders.

Day Trips:

Use Interlaken as a base to explore the Jungfrau Region, including Grindelwald, Lauterbrunnen, and the Jungfraujoch.

Tips for Visiting:

Adventure activities can be weather-dependent, so plan a flexible schedule.

The Swiss Travel Pass can save money if you're using trains and boats frequently.

Summer and early fall are the best times for outdoor activities and clear views.

Lucerne and Lake Lucerne

Lucerne is one of Switzerland's most picturesque cities, known for its preserved medieval architecture, lakeside setting, and dramatic mountain views. Nestled along the shores of Lake Lucerne, the city is a perfect blend of tradition and modernity. It's an ideal base for exploring central Switzerland, whether you're interested in culture, nature, or boat cruises.

Location:
Lucerne is in central Switzerland, easily accessible from Zurich (about an hour by train). It sits on the northwest shore of Lake Lucerne and is surrounded by Alpine peaks like Mount Pilatus and Mount Rigi.

History:
Founded in the 8th century, Lucerne rose to importance as a trading center during the Middle Ages. It joined the Swiss Confederation in the 14th century and has retained much of its historical charm, with landmarks like the Chapel Bridge and Musegg Wall showcasing its heritage.

Opening and Closing Hours:
The city and lake are always accessible. Specific attractions, such as museums, cable cars, and boat services, generally operate between 9:00 AM and 6:00 PM, with variations by season.

Switzerland Travel Guide 2025`

Top Things to Do:

Chapel Bridge (Kapellbrücke):

This 14th-century wooden bridge is Lucerne's most iconic site, complete with painted panels and a historic tower.

Lake Lucerne Boat Cruise:

Take a steamboat or modern vessel across the lake to towns like Weggis or Brunnen, surrounded by scenic mountain landscapes.

Mount Pilatus or Mount Rigi Excursion:

Ride the world's steepest cogwheel railway to Mount Pilatus, or take a boat and cable car combo to Mount Rigi for incredible views.

Musegg Wall:

Walk along the preserved medieval walls of Lucerne, some of which still have functioning clock towers.

Swiss Museum of Transport:

One of Switzerland's most visited museums, it covers everything from trains and planes to space travel and media.

Tips for Visiting:

Purchase a day pass for Lake Lucerne cruises to hop between lakeside towns.

Visit early or late in the day for fewer crowds at popular sites.

Combine a boat ride with a mountain excursion for a full-day round trip.

The Swiss National Park

The Swiss National Park is Switzerland's only national park and the oldest in the Alps, offering untouched nature, wildlife spotting, and pristine hiking trails. It's a protected sanctuary dedicated to preserving Alpine ecosystems.

Location:
Located in the canton of Graubünden in eastern Switzerland, near the town of Zernez. The park covers over 170 square kilometers in the Engadine Valley.

History:
Established in 1914, the Swiss National Park was one of Europe's first national parks. It was created to serve as a strict nature reserve, where ecosystems are left undisturbed. The park follows strict guidelines—visitors must stick to marked trails, and no camping, fires, or picking plants is allowed.

Opening and Closing Hours:

Open Year-Round, but access is best from **June to October** when trails are free of snow.

Visitor Centre in Zernez:

Summer: 8:30 AM – 6:00 PM

Winter: 9:00 AM – 5:00 PM

Closed on some public holidays.

Top Things to Do:

Hiking:
There are over 80 km of marked trails, ranging from easy walks to more challenging alpine hikes. The trails are well-maintained and clearly signposted.

Wildlife Watching:

Spot animals like ibex, marmots, golden eagles, and red deer. Early mornings and evenings offer the best chances.

Visit the National Park Centre in Zernez:

Interactive exhibits explain the park's ecosystems, flora, and fauna, ideal for families and educational visits.

Photography and Birdwatching:
Bring binoculars or a zoom lens to capture the diverse landscapes and elusive wildlife.

Tips for Visiting:

Stick to marked trails; leaving paths is strictly forbidden.

Pack food and water, as there are no restaurants or shops inside the park.

Dress appropriately—weather can shift quickly in the Alps.

No pets, drones, or bikes are allowed.

Zurich

Zurich is Switzerland's largest city, a global financial hub with a lively arts scene, historic Old Town, upscale shopping, and a vibrant lakefront. It combines urban sophistication with access to natural beauty, making it a great starting or ending point for a Swiss vacation.

Location:
Located in northern Switzerland on the shores of Lake Zurich and at the foot of the Alps. The city is a major transportation hub with direct train, car, and flight connections to all of Europe.

History:
Zurich was originally a Roman customs post known as *Turicum*. It became a Free Imperial City in the Holy Roman Empire and later joined the Swiss Confederation. By the 16th century, it was a center for the Protestant Reformation under Ulrich Zwingli. Today, it is a cultural and economic powerhouse.

Opening and Closing Hours:

City is always accessible.

Most museums: **10:00 AM – 5:00 PM (Tuesday to Sunday)**; many are closed on Mondays.

Shops: **9:00 AM – 6:30 PM (Monday to Saturday)**; closed on Sundays.

Restaurants and bars generally open until **10:00 PM – midnight**.

Top Things to Do:

Old Town (Altstadt):

Wander through cobbled alleys lined with medieval buildings, boutique shops, and cafes. Key landmarks include Grossmünster, Fraumünster, and St. Peter's Church.

Lake Zurich Cruise or Walk:

Take a relaxing boat ride or stroll along the lake promenade for beautiful city and mountain views.

Bahnhofstrasse:
One of the world's most exclusive shopping streets, offering everything from luxury brands to Swiss watches and chocolates.

Kunsthaus Zürich and Swiss National Museum:

Explore world-class art collections and learn about Swiss history and culture.

Uetliberg Mountain:

Hike or take a train to the top for panoramic views of the entire Zurich region and the Alps.

Tips for Visiting:

Zurich is expensive—opt for city passes that include public transport and discounts to attractions.

Many museums offer free or discounted entry on specific days.

Use Zurich as a base for day trips to Lucerne, Rhine Falls, or Appenzell.

Chapter 7: Natural Wonders and Landscapes

The Swiss Alps: Hiking, Skiing, and Panoramas

The Swiss Alps are the soul of Switzerland—home to dramatic peaks, alpine lakes, glacier-fed rivers, and postcard-worthy villages. Whether you're visiting in summer or winter, the Alps offer unforgettable experiences.

Hiking in the Swiss Alps

Best Season: Late June to mid-October (snow-free trails and full hut service)

Trail Options:

Easy: 5 Lakes Walk (Zermatt), Panoramaweg near Grindelwald, or the Aletsch Glacier Viewpoint hike

Moderate: Eiger Trail (below the Eiger North Face), Oeschinensee Lake trail, Schynige Platte to First

Challenging: Haute Route (Zermatt to Chamonix), Via Alpina, and sections of the Tour du Mont Blanc

Tips:

Use the **SwitzerlandMobility** app or local tourist maps for accurate trail info

Wear proper hiking shoes and pack for weather changes—even in summer

Skiing in the Swiss Alps

Best Season: Late November to April (longer at higher altitudes like Zermatt or Saas-Fee)

Top Ski Resorts:

Zermatt: Skiing year-round on the glacier, plus Matterhorn views

St. Moritz: Glamour, snow polo, and over 300 km of runs

Verbier: Part of the 4 Vallées—ideal for advanced skiers

Davos-Klosters: Great for families and off-piste skiing

Grindelwald-Wengen: Scenic Jungfrau backdrop, accessible and family-friendly

Ski Pass Tips:

Multi-resort passes like the **Swiss Ski Pass** or regional options offer good value for extended stays

Panoramas and Alpine Experiences

Best Viewing Platforms:

Jungfraujoch (Top of Europe): Europe's highest railway station at 3,454m

Gornergrat: Sweeping views of 29 peaks over 4,000m, including the Matterhorn

Schilthorn: Revolving restaurant made famous by James Bond

Titlis: Cliff walk and glacier cave

Harder Kulm (Interlaken): Quick and scenic, with lakes and Alps visible from one spot

Iconic Mountains: Matterhorn, Eiger, and Jungfrau

Matterhorn (4,478 m) – The Most Photographed Mountain in the World

Location: Near Zermatt, Valais region

Why It's Famous: Its sharp, pyramidal shape has become a national symbol (and inspired the Toblerone chocolate shape)

Best Views: Gornergrat, Stellisee Lake, and Rothorn Paradise

Climbing: One of the most challenging climbs in the Alps—only for experienced mountaineers with guides

Nearby Experiences: Matterhorn Glacier Paradise (Europe's highest cable car station), summer skiing, alpine lakes

Eiger (3,967 m) – The Fearsome North Face

Location: Bernese Oberland, near Grindelwald

Why It's Famous: The "Eiger Nordwand" (North Face) is a legendary, deadly climb known for mountaineering history and danger

Best Views: Kleine Scheidegg, Eiger Trail, or from the train to Jungfraujoch

Climbing: Technical and notorious—attempts are only for elite climbers

Hiking Tip: The **Eiger Trail** offers incredible up-close views of the face without risk

Jungfrau (4,158 m) – The Maiden of the Alps

Location: Bernese Alps, between the cantons of Bern and Valais

Why It's Famous: Part of the iconic Eiger–Mönch–Jungfrau trio; home to the Jungfraujoch station and Aletsch Glacier

Best Views: From Lauterbrunnen Valley, Wengen, or the Sphinx Observatory at Jungfraujoch

Experiences: Snow fun park, glacier hikes, Ice Palace, and UNESCO-listed landscapes

Travel Tips for Visiting the Iconic Peaks

Get an Early Start: Mornings offer the best light and clearest skies

Book in Advance: For mountain trains and cable cars like Jungfraujoch and Gornergrat, especially in high season

Bundle Passes: Consider the **Swiss Travel Pass**, **Berner Oberland Regional Pass**, or **Matterhorn Gotthard Pass** for savings

Weather: Always check live webcams and forecasts—weather can change dramatically at altitude

Lakes of Switzerland: Geneva, Lucerne, Zurich, and More

Switzerland's lakes are as iconic as its mountains, offering not just beauty, but recreation, boat tours, swimming, and lakeside towns filled with charm.

Lake Geneva (Lac Léman)

Location: Western Switzerland, bordering France

Highlights:

The Jet d'Eau in Geneva

Lavaux Vineyards (UNESCO-listed, great for wine lovers)

Chillon Castle near Montreux

Lakeside promenades in Lausanne, Vevey, and Nyon

Activities: Boat cruises, wine tastings, paddleboarding, cultural festivals (e.g., Montreux Jazz Festival)

Lake Lucerne

Location: Central Switzerland

Highlights:

Surrounded by mountains like Pilatus and Rigi

Historic paddle steamers and scenic boat rides

Chapel Bridge and Lucerne Old Town

Activities: Lake cruises, swimming spots, hiking the Swiss Path, visiting lakeside villages like Weggis and Vitznau

Lake Zurich

Location: Eastern Switzerland

Highlights:

Zurich's lakeside promenades and public "badis" (swimming areas)

Ferry rides between towns like Küsnacht, Rapperswil, and Meilen

Activities: Urban swimming, boat rentals, dining cruises, lakeside cycling trails

Other Notable Lakes:

Lake Thun & Lake Brienz (Interlaken): Turquoise waters, mountain reflections, perfect for kayaking and boat tours

Lake Maggiore & Lake Lugano (Ticino): Mediterranean ambiance, palm trees, lakeside towns with Italian flair

Lake Oeschinen (Bernese Oberland): Glacial mountain lake, ideal for hiking, swimming, and picnics

Lake Cauma & Lake Cresta (Graubünden): Crystal-clear, forest-surrounded alpine lakes, loved for summer swims

Waterfalls, Gorges, and Caves

Switzerland's rugged geography means you'll find some of Europe's most impressive natural features—from roaring waterfalls to deep gorges and mysterious caves.

Waterfalls

Rhine Falls – *Europe's Largest Waterfall*

Location: Near Schaffhausen

Height: 23 meters, but very wide and powerful

Experience: Take a boat to the rock in the middle or walk along viewing platforms

Best Time: Late spring/early summer when snowmelt swells the river

Staubbach Falls – *Lauterbrunnen's Iconic Drop*

Location: Lauterbrunnen Valley

Height: ~300 meters

Experience: Visible from almost everywhere in the valley; a path leads behind the fall in summer

Trümmelbach Falls – *Glacier-fed and Inside a Mountain*

Location: Lauterbrunnen Valley

Highlights: 10 glacier waterfalls inside a mountain, accessible by lifts and tunnels

Open: April to November

Reichenbach Falls – *Famous for Sherlock Holmes*

Location: Meiringen

Trivia: Where Holmes and Moriarty had their legendary fall

Access: By funicular, walking trail, or scenic path

Gorges (Schluchten)

Aare Gorge (Aareschlucht)

Location: Near Meiringen

Features: Walk on wooden pathways through a narrow limestone gorge carved by the Aare River

Open: Late March to early November

Rosenlaui Glacier Gorge

Location: Near Grindelwald

Highlights: Turquoise waters, waterfalls, narrow passages, and rock formations

Experience: Easy walk but incredibly scenic

Gorner Gorge

Location: Near Zermatt

Features: Green-tinged river water rushing between steep rock walls

Best Time: Late spring through early fall

Caves

St. Beatus Caves

Location: Near Lake Thun

Legends: Said to be once inhabited by a dragon

Highlights: Lit pathways through stalactites, underground lakes, and a small museum

Good For: Families and rainy day activities

Höllgrotten Caves

Location: Near Baar (Zug area)

Features: Colorfully lit limestone caverns with stalactites and fairy-tale ambiance

Access: Easy short trail through the forest to the entrance

Lac Souterrain de St-Léonard

Location: Valais region

Unique For: Europe's largest underground lake

Experience: Guided boat ride through crystal-clear waters in an underground chamber

Travel Tips:

Dress Appropriately: Even in summer, caves and gorges can be cool and damp

Safety: Watch your step—some gorge trails can be slippery, especially after rain

Timing: Visit early or late in the day to avoid peak tourist crowds at major waterfalls

Combinations: Pair waterfalls or lakes with scenic train journeys like the Bernina Express or GoldenPass Line

National Parks and Nature Reserves

Switzerland's landscapes are protected through a network of national parks, regional nature parks, and reserves that preserve alpine ecosystems, biodiversity, and traditional ways of life.

1. Swiss National Park (Graubünden)

Switzerland's only official national park, and the oldest in the Alps (est. 1914).

A strict nature reserve: no camping, fires, or off-trail walking.

Best for: Wildlife spotting (ibex, marmots, golden eagles), high alpine hikes, unspoiled nature.

Top Trail: Margunet Trail – scenic and family-friendly with panoramic views.

2. Parc Ela (Graubünden)

Largest nature park in Switzerland by area.

Combines natural beauty with cultural villages and historic trails.

Highlights: Albula Pass, Roman roads, scenic villages like Bergün and Savognin.

3. Binntal Nature Park (Valais)

Known for rare minerals, tranquil hikes, and traditional architecture.

Unique Feature: Over 200 types of minerals found in this region.

Activities: Guided geo-hikes and visits to old mine galleries.

4. Regional Nature Parks

Switzerland is home to 19 recognized regional parks, including:

Gruyère Pays-d'Enhaut (cheese production, alpine pastures)

Gantrisch Nature Park (close to Bern, with easy access for day hikes)

Val Müstair Biosphere Reserve (UNESCO-listed, blends cultural heritage and alpine wilderness)

Chapter 8: Swiss Culture and Traditions

Languages and Regional Difference

Switzerland is a multilingual nation with four official languages and distinct cultural zones that reflect its European neighbors. Understanding these differences will enrich your travel experience.

1. The Four National Languages

German (spoken by ~62% of the population)

Dominates the central and eastern regions

Dialect: *Swiss German* (Schweizerdeutsch) is common in speech but standard High German is used in writing, signs, and formal situations

French (~23%)

Spoken in western Switzerland (Romandy)

Cantons: Geneva, Vaud, Neuchâtel, Jura, parts of Valais and Fribourg

Italian (~8%)

Spoken in southern Switzerland, mainly the canton of Ticino and parts of southern Graubünden

Culture and cuisine have strong Mediterranean influence

Romansh (~0.5%)

Spoken in parts of canton Graubünden

A Romance language with several dialects; protected as a national language and symbol of Swiss heritage

2. Regional Cultural Zones

German-Speaking Switzerland (Deutschschweiz)

Cities: Zurich, Bern, Lucerne, Basel

Switzerland Travel Guide 2025`

More reserved, efficient, and organized

Strong tradition of precision, industry, and alpine sports

French-Speaking Switzerland (Suisse Romande)

Cities: Geneva, Lausanne, Neuchâtel

More relaxed vibe, elegant lakefronts, wine culture

Greater influence from French cuisine and art

Italian-Speaking Switzerland (Svizzera italiana)

City: Lugano

Warm hospitality, vibrant piazzas, rich cuisine

Italian customs blended with Swiss structure

Romansh Region

Villages: Scuol, Disentis, Flims

Preserves mountain traditions, local music, and rural customs

Strong Alpine identity and connection to nature

Travel Tips

English is widely understood in tourist areas

Learn a few basic greetings in the local language—it's always appreciated

Be mindful that regional customs vary (e.g., greeting with handshakes vs. cheek kisses)

Swiss Festivals and Events (2025 Calendar)

Switzerland offers a vibrant lineup of cultural, music, food, and seasonal festivals year-round. Here's a curated list of the most notable events to catch in 2025:

Winter & Spring

January – Lauberhorn Ski Races (Wengen)

One of the world's longest and oldest ski races; combines thrilling sports with village charm.

February – Basel Fasnacht (Carnival)

A UNESCO-recognized event with masked parades, "Morgestraich" lantern processions, and confetti-filled streets.

March – Geneva International Motor Show

A major event in the automotive world, showcasing the latest car innovations.

April – Cully Jazz Festival (Vaud)

Held along Lake Geneva's Lavaux vineyards, this intimate jazz festival blends music with wine tastings.

Summer

June – Art Basel (Basel)

The world's premier modern and contemporary art fair; attracts galleries, collectors, and artists from around the globe.

July – Montreux Jazz Festival (Lake Geneva)

One of Europe's biggest music festivals, with global headliners and lakeside performances.

July – Fête de l'Escalade (Geneva)

Historical reenactments, medieval parades, and traditional chocolate cauldrons mark this local favorite.

August 1 – Swiss National Day

Celebrated across the country with fireworks, speeches, parades, and traditional foods.

August – Locarno Film Festival (Ticino)

One of Europe's top open-air film events, held in a picturesque Italian-speaking town.

Autumn & Winter

September – Alpabfahrt / Désalpe Festivals

Cow parades through towns as herders bring livestock down from alpine pastures; music, cheese, and flowers abound (held in various regions).

October – Geneva Chocolate Festival

Celebrate Swiss chocolate with artisan tastings, workshops, and pairings with wine and coffee.

November – Onion Market (Zibelemärit) in Bern

A fun, quirky event with onion braids, confetti, and local specialties.

December – Christmas Markets

Zurich, Basel, Montreux, and Lucerne host some of the best

Expect mulled wine, handmade gifts, Alpine treats, and festive ambiance

Travel Tips:

Plan ahead: Major festivals require hotel bookings months in advance.

Check regional calendars: Smaller village festivals often offer rich cultural experiences without the crowds.

Bundle transport: Use a **Swiss Travel Pass** for easy rail access to festivals across the country.

Alpine Folklore and Music

Switzerland's Alpine folklore is a rich tapestry of myths, pastoral traditions, seasonal rituals, and music that has been passed down for centuries—especially in the mountain regions of central and eastern Switzerland.

Key Elements of Swiss Folklore

Legendary Creatures and Stories:

Tales of dragons (like in St. Beatus Caves), mountain spirits, and helpful dwarfs are part of rural oral history.

The **Wildmannli** (wild man) is a common mythological figure said to roam the forests and mountains.

Yodeling (Jodeln):

A form of singing with rapid changes in pitch that originated in the Alps as a way to communicate across valleys.

Still performed at folk festivals, especially in central and eastern Switzerland (Appenzell, Bernese Oberland).

Often accompanied by the **accordion** or **alphorn**.

Alphorn Music:

A long, wooden horn traditionally used by herdsmen in the Alps to call cattle or communicate across distances.

Now a symbol of Swiss heritage, featured in cultural events, tourism showcases, and national holidays.

Folk Dancing:

Regional dances include the "Schottisch" and "Ländler," performed in pairs to accordion or fiddle music.

Folk dance clubs and festivals keep these traditions alive, often inviting audience participation.

Cowbells (Treicheln):

Used historically to locate livestock in alpine pastures.

Now a musical instrument and souvenir; prominent in **Alpabfahrt** parades where cows return from high pastures in decorated splendor.

Where to Experience It:

Appenzell, Grindelwald, and **Zermatt**: Folk music festivals, open-air concerts, and traditional events.

Unspunnen Festival (Interlaken): Held every 12 years; features yodeling, wrestling, and other folk traditions.

Traditional Clothing and Customs

Swiss traditional dress—*Tracht*—varies by canton and reflects a deep sense of regional identity, often worn during festivals, parades, weddings, and folk events.

Men's Traditional Clothing

Components:

Embroidered vests or jackets (often red or black)

White shirts with puffed sleeves

Knee-length breeches or woolen trousers

Wide belts and hats (sometimes adorned with feathers or edelweiss)

Special Note: In Appenzell, men wear ornate silver jewelry and a ceremonial sword during parades.

Women's Traditional Clothing

Components:

Blouses with puffed sleeves and lace trim

Colorful skirts with aprons, often embroidered

Corset-style bodices with metal or ribbon fastenings

Lace or linen caps (some highly detailed depending on the region)

Regional Differences

Appenzell: Known for its highly decorative clothing with silver and gold elements

Ticino: Lighter, more Mediterranean-inspired attire with floral designs

Valais: Darker, more reserved tones, often including edelweiss motifs

Bernese Oberland: Dresses with detailed lacework and leather accessories

Customs Still Practiced Today

Alpabfahrt / Désalpe: Cows wear flower crowns and farmers don traditional outfits while leading herds back to the valley in autumn.

Swiss National Day (August 1st): Folk dress, alphorn performances, and flag-waving ceremonies are common.

Jodlerfeste: Yodeling festivals where traditional attire is proudly worn and regional teams compete in music and dance.

Travel Tips:

Visit a Museum: The Swiss Open-Air Museum Ballenberg (near Interlaken) showcases traditional houses and costumes from all regions.

Attend Local Events: Ask your hotel or tourist office about nearby festivals, wrestling matches (*Schwingen*), or musical gatherings.

Buy Ethically Made Souvenirs: Many artisans still handcraft traditional clothing and instruments using ancestral techniques.

Understanding Swiss Neutrality and Civic Pride

Swiss Neutrality: A Historic Pillar

Switzerland's neutrality is one of its most defining national traits—an enduring political stance that shapes its foreign policy, defense, and identity.

Origins and Evolution

Historical Roots: Swiss neutrality dates back to the early 19th century, formally recognized by the Congress of Vienna in 1815.

World Wars: Switzerland maintained neutrality during both WWI and WWII, avoiding direct involvement while supporting humanitarian efforts (e.g., Red Cross operations).

Modern Day: Switzerland is not part of military alliances like NATO and is not a member of the EU, though it maintains close economic and diplomatic ties.

What It Means in Practice

No Military Entanglements: Switzerland does not participate in foreign conflicts or alliances.

International Mediator: Often serves as a host for peace negotiations and global diplomacy (e.g., Geneva hosts UN agencies and summits).

Compulsory Military Service: Despite neutrality, the country maintains a strong defense force, primarily for protection and civil aid.

Civic Pride and National Identity

Switzerland has a unique form of national pride grounded in:

Direct Democracy: Citizens regularly vote on laws via referendums—sometimes up to four times per year.

Cantonal Autonomy: Each of the 26 cantons has significant independence, fostering strong local identities.

Respect for Rules and Precision: Seen in punctual public transport, clean cities, and efficient bureaucracy.

Multilingual Harmony: Despite linguistic and regional diversity, Switzerland thrives through mutual respect and shared values.

Symbols of Civic Pride

Swiss Flag: Red with a white cross, representing peace and neutrality.

National Day (August 1st): Celebrated with fireworks, bonfires, and speeches highlighting unity and heritage.

Alphorns and Cowbells: Not just tourist attractions—symbols of connection to the land and history.

Chapter 9: Outdoor Adventures and Activities

Skiing & Snowboarding Resorts

Switzerland is a global leader in winter sports, with world-class ski resorts, reliable snowfall, scenic alpine villages, and high-quality infrastructure. Whether you're a beginner or an expert skier, there's a perfect slope waiting for you.

Top Ski Resorts (2025 Update)

1. Zermatt

Highlight: Views of the Matterhorn, year-round skiing on the glacier

Slopes: 360+ km of ski runs, connected to Cervinia (Italy)

Extras: Car-free village, luxury chalets, top-rated après-ski

Best for: All skill levels, scenic skiing, and advanced snowboarding

2. St. Moritz

Highlight: Glamorous, elite resort with Olympic heritage

Slopes: 350+ km of pistes, high-altitude reliability

Extras: Designer shops, gourmet dining, polo on ice

Best for: Experienced skiers and luxury travelers

3. Verbier (4 Vallées)

Highlight: Largest ski area in Switzerland

Slopes: Over 400 km of terrain, epic freeride zones

Extras: Lively nightlife, international vibe

Best for: Advanced skiers, social scene seekers

4. Davos-Klosters

Highlight: One of the highest towns in Europe

Slopes: 300 km of ski runs, variety of ski areas

Extras: Excellent for families and snowboarders

Best for: Mixed groups, long ski trips

5. Grindelwald-Wengen (Jungfrau Region)

Highlight: Unmatched views of the Eiger, Mönch & Jungfrau

Slopes: 200+ km, great for intermediate levels

Extras: Cogwheel train rides, alpine villages

Best for: Scenic skiing, beginners to intermediates

Tips for Ski Season

When to Go: Late December to March is peak season

Swiss Travel Pass: Offers discounts on ski lifts and mountain railways

Book Early: Resorts fill quickly—book accommodations and ski passes months in advance

Equipment Rental: Available at every resort with modern gear and multilingual staff

Hiking Trails and Alpine Routes

When the snow melts, Switzerland transforms into a hiker's paradise, with thousands of kilometers of marked trails through valleys, mountains, and pastures.

Top Hiking Regions and Trails

1. The Bernese Oberland

Trail: *Eiger Trail* (Grindelwald to Alpiglen)

Length: ~6 km, 2 hours

Highlights: Close-up views of the Eiger's North Face

2. Zermatt Region

Trail: *Five Lakes Walk (5-Seenweg)*

Length: ~10 km, 3 hours

Highlights: Lakes reflecting the Matterhorn, perfect for photos

3. Lauterbrunnen Valley

Trail: *Valley Walk to Trümmelbach Falls*

Length: Easy 2-3 km walk

Highlights: 72 waterfalls, Swiss chalets, dramatic cliffs

4. Engadin (St. Moritz Area)

Trail: *Muottas Muragl to Alp Languard*

Length: ~7 km

Highlights: Panoramic views over lakes and peaks, suitable for moderate hikers

5. Ticino (Italian-speaking Region)

Trail: *Verzasca Valley Trail*

Length: 12+ km

Highlights: Emerald rivers, Roman bridges, rustic stone villages

Long-Distance Routes

Via Alpina: 390 km trail crossing Switzerland east to west

Swiss National Route 1 (Trans-Swiss Trail): Connects Porrentruy to Mendrisio

Chemin de Saint-Jacques: Swiss portion of the Camino de Santiago

Tips for Hiking Season

Best Time: Late May to October (depending on altitude)

Trail Markings:

Yellow signs: Easy trails

Red and white: Mountain trails (moderate)

Blue and white: Alpine routes (challenging)

Gear Up: Bring good shoes, layers, water, and sun protection

Use Swiss Mobility App: For trail maps, weather updates, and transport links

Paragliding, Ziplining, and Skydiving

Switzerland's dramatic landscapes make it one of Europe's top destinations for aerial adventures, offering unparalleled views of mountains, lakes, and valleys.

Paragliding

Top Spots for Paragliding

Interlaken – Known as the adventure capital of Switzerland. Tandem flights over Lake Thun, Lake Brienz, and the Jungfrau massif.

Zermatt – Fly with the Matterhorn as your backdrop.

Lucerne – Launch from Mount Pilatus or Rigi for panoramic lake views.

Verbier – High-altitude flights with experienced pilots.

Good to Know

No experience needed: Tandem flights with licensed pilots are beginner-friendly.

Best Season: April to October, though winter paragliding is also available in some regions.

Costs: Expect CHF 150–250 for tandem flights depending on altitude and location.

Ziplining

Notable Zipline Parks

First Cliff Walk (Grindelwald) – Includes the **First Flyer**, a 800-meter zipline at high speed.

Saas-Fee – Offers the *Feeblitz* alpine zipline coaster and adventure park.

Rope Parks – Found in Zermatt, Arosa, and Davos with ziplines integrated into forest circuits.

Why Try It?

Great family activity

Often combined with suspension bridges and treetop walks

Safe, supervised, and scenic

Skydiving

Where to Skydive in Switzerland

Interlaken – Most popular location; offers jumps from helicopters or planes with views of the Eiger, Mönch, and Jungfrau.

Lauterbrunnen – A dramatic valley surrounded by sheer cliffs—stunning visuals guaranteed.

Locarno – Skydiving above lakes and palm-lined towns in southern Switzerland.

Details

Altitude: 4,000–4,600 meters (13,000–15,000 feet)

Jump Type: Tandem or solo (with certification)

Cost: CHF 400–500 for tandem skydives including photos/videos

Mountain Biking and Climbing

Switzerland's terrain is ideal for both mountain biking and climbing, offering trails and routes for all skill levels with incredible alpine scenery.

Mountain Biking

Top Regions

Graubünden (e.g., Davos, Lenzerheide) – Famous for long downhill tracks, bike parks, and cable car-accessed trails.

Zermatt – Scenic rides at the foot of the Matterhorn; e-bike routes available.

Engadin (St. Moritz) – Network of high-altitude trails, both technical and scenic.

Valais – Offers 1,300 km of marked trails with wine-region views and glacier passes.

Highlights

Bike Parks: Lenzerheide and Davos offer some of the best downhill infrastructure in the country.

E-Bikes: Widely available for rent—ideal for beginners or long-distance trips.

Season: Mid-May to late October (depending on snow levels)

Climbing

Best Climbing Locations

Jura Mountains – Limestone cliffs, ideal for beginners and sport climbing.

Grimsel Pass – Granite walls and scenic alpine climbs for experienced climbers.

Engelberg and Churfirsten – Popular for traditional and multi-pitch routes.

Via Ferrata Routes:

Mürren-Gimmelwald: Fixed cables and ladders along vertical cliffs.

Saas-Fee Gorge Alpine Route: A mix of hiking, scrambling, and climbing.

Indoor Options

Climbing Gyms in major cities like Zurich, Geneva, and Lausanne are available year-round for training or rainy-day alternatives.

Adventure Travel Tips

Guides Available: Many towns offer local guides for mountain sports, especially for climbing and skydiving.

Safety First: Always check weather conditions, and use licensed operators for all aerial activities.

Insurance: Make sure your travel insurance covers extreme sports and mountain rescue.

Winter vs Summer Activities

Switzerland transforms into a snowy wonderland ideal for winter sports and cozy mountain escapes.

Top Activities

Skiing & Snowboarding

Renowned resorts: Zermatt, Verbier, St. Moritz, Davos, and Grindelwald

Suitable for all skill levels, with well-maintained pistes and lifts

Snowshoeing & Winter Hiking

Peaceful trails through forests and mountain valleys, like those around Arosa or the Engadine

Sledding (Tobogganing)

Scenic runs in places like Bergün, Preda, or Mürren

Ice Skating

Outdoor rinks in Zurich, Lausanne, and even on frozen lakes (e.g., Lake Davos)

Wellness & Spas

Relax in thermal baths like Leukerbad, or mountaintop spas with panoramic views

Christmas Markets & Winter Festivals

Atmospheric events in Basel, Montreux, and Lucerne with crafts, food, and mulled wine

Summer Activities (June to September)

As the snow melts, Switzerland reveals green valleys, blooming meadows, and hiking-friendly peaks.

Top Activities

Hiking & Trekking

Hundreds of marked trails, from lakeside paths to high alpine routes (e.g., the Five Lakes Walk near Zermatt)

Swimming & Lake Activities

Swim, paddleboard, or cruise on lakes like Geneva, Lucerne, and Brienz

Scenic Train Rides

Bernina Express and Glacier Express are more accessible and offer lush summer views

Paragliding & Adventure Sports

Soar over Interlaken or Lauterbrunnen with snow-capped peaks in the distance

Mountain Festivals & Local Events

Celebrate Swiss culture, cheese-making, and traditional crafts in alpine villages

Cycling & Mountain Biking

Cool weather and spectacular backdrops make summer perfect for riding

Mountain Biking and Climbing

Switzerland's alpine geography is a paradise for outdoor sports enthusiasts, offering some of Europe's best terrain for mountain biking and climbing.

Mountain Biking in Switzerland

Switzerland has an extensive network of biking trails, ranging from gentle countryside routes to adrenaline-pumping downhill tracks.

Popular Mountain Biking Regions

Graubünden

Over 700 km of trails, including the legendary *Alps Epic Trail Davos*

Lift-assisted biking and alpine huts for overnight stays

Valais

Trails near Verbier, Zermatt, and Crans-Montana

Mix of forest trails, alpine ridges, and flow trails

Ticino

Combine mountain biking with lake views and Italian-style villages

Engadine

High-altitude trails with glacier views and wildlife sightings

Bike Infrastructure

Many resorts offer:

Bike transport on cable cars

Rental and repair shops

Marked trails by skill level (easy, intermediate, expert)

Rock and Alpine Climbing

Switzerland offers something for every level of climber—from bouldering parks to world-class alpine ascents.

Climbing Options

Sport Climbing

Crags like *San Paolo* (Ticino) or *Gastlosen* (Bernese Oberland)

Multi-Pitch Climbing

Classic routes in Grimsel, Furka, or in the Valais region

Alpine Climbing

Iconic peaks like the **Matterhorn**, **Eiger**, and **Dufourspitze** (Switzerland's highest)

Requires technical experience or guided tours

Via Ferrata

Secure climbing paths with cables and ladders (e.g., Murren or Leukerbad routes)

Suitable for beginners with a head for heights

Climbing Tips

Always check weather and avalanche reports

Book certified guides for high-alpine climbs

Consider insurance that covers mountain rescue

Switzerland Travel Guide 2025`

Winter vs Summer Activities

Switzerland is a true year-round destination, offering dramatically different outdoor experiences depending on the season. Here's how to make the most of both:

Winter Activities (December to March)

Switzerland transforms into a snowy paradise perfect for winter sports, cozy villages, and festive magic.

Top Winter Experiences

Skiing & Snowboarding

World-class resorts: Zermatt, Verbier, St. Moritz, Davos, and Grindelwald

Slopes for all skill levels, plus ski schools and après-ski culture

Winter Hiking & Snowshoeing

Scenic trails through snow-covered forests and mountain ridges

Popular areas: Engadin Valley, Goms, and Arosa

Tobogganing (Sledging)

Family-friendly runs in places like Bergün and Grindelwald-First

Christmas Markets & Festivals

Magical markets in Zurich, Basel, Lucerne, and Montreux

Mulled wine, festive lights, and local crafts

Thermal Baths & Spas

Ideal for relaxing in snow-covered settings: Leukerbad, Vals, and Bad Ragaz

Ice Skating & Ice Climbing

Public rinks in cities and natural lakes in alpine areas

Ice climbing tours in frozen waterfalls for thrill-seekers

Switzerland Travel Guide 2025`

Summer Activities (June to September)

When the snow melts, the Swiss outdoors burst into color—perfect for hiking, biking, and lake adventures.

Top Summer Experiences

Hiking & Trekking

Over 65,000 km of marked trails

Iconic routes: Eiger Trail, Five Lakes Walk (Zermatt), Via Alpina

Lake Swimming & Boating

Clean, swimmable lakes like Lake Geneva, Lake Zurich, and Lake Lucerne

Paddleboarding, kayaking, and sailing options

Paragliding & Skydiving

Soar over Interlaken or Lauterbrunnen for breathtaking alpine views

Open-Air Festivals

Montreux Jazz Festival, Paléo Festival Nyon, and village folklore events

Alpine Flower Watching & Picnics

Meadows in full bloom, especially around Grindelwald and Appenzell

Glacier Excursions

Summer hikes or cable car rides to glaciers like Aletsch and Titlis

Chapter 10: Food and Drink in Switzerland

Traditional Swiss Cuisine

1. Fondue

Fondue is one of the most famous and beloved Swiss dishes, originating from the French-speaking region of Switzerland. It consists of a rich, creamy cheese sauce made from melted Swiss cheeses, traditionally Gruyère and Emmental. The dish is served in a communal pot, and pieces of bread are dipped into the melted cheese using long forks.

Taste
The taste of fondue is rich, savory, and creamy, with the distinct flavors of Gruyère and Emmental coming through. The wine and garlic used in the preparation add subtle complexity to the cheese mixture, making it a decadent treat.

Preparation
Fondue is typically made by melting cheese with white wine (such as a dry Swiss white wine like Chasselas) and a little bit of kirsch (cherry brandy). Garlic is

rubbed onto the pot, then the cheese and wine mixture is gently heated until smooth. The dish is served with cubes of bread, which are speared with forks and dipped into the cheese.

Where to Try

Château de Chillon (Montreux): An atmospheric castle where you can enjoy fondue with a view of Lake Geneva.

Restaurant Le Gruyérien (Geneva): A cozy spot offering traditional Swiss fondue.

Fondue Chalet (Zurich): A fun place where you can experience a traditional Swiss fondue dinner.

What Makes it Iconic?

Fondue is iconic because it represents Swiss communal dining and their love for cheese. It's a social meal, where family and friends gather around a pot, sharing food and enjoying each other's company. It's also a comforting, rich dish that has stood the test of time.

Tips for Enjoying

Avoid stirring the cheese fondue too much, as this can cause it to become stringy.

If you drop your bread in the pot, tradition says you must buy a round of drinks for everyone at the table!

Pair with a glass of white wine or hot tea, and remember to dip in bread, not too much at once to avoid splashing.

2. Raclette

Raclette is both a type of cheese and a traditional Swiss dish. It involves melting the Raclette cheese and scraping it off onto potatoes, pickles, onions, and sometimes meat. This dish is often associated with the Valais region.

Taste
Raclette cheese is semi-hard, with a buttery, slightly nutty flavor. When melted, it becomes creamy and gooey, which pairs wonderfully with the boiled potatoes and the acidity of the pickles.

Preparation
The cheese is heated until it melts, usually in a raclette grill or under a special heat source. The melted cheese is then scraped onto the accompaniments like potatoes, vegetables, and cured meats.

Where to Try

Chez Maman Raclette (Geneva): A place that specializes in raclette served in a traditional setting.

Restaurant Le Vieux Chalet (Zermatt): Perfect for enjoying raclette with an Alpine backdrop.

The Raclette Bar (Zurich): A charming place offering traditional raclette with a variety of sides.

What Makes it Iconic?

Raclette is iconic because it's a dish steeped in tradition, with roots in the alpine regions where it was originally consumed by herders. It has become synonymous with Swiss comfort food.

Tips for Enjoying

Don't skimp on the accompaniments—pickles, onions, and meats balance the richness of the cheese.

Use a raclette grill at home for the full experience. It's a fun and interactive way to enjoy the dish.

Avoid overcooking the cheese—keep it gooey and melt it to perfection.

3. Älplermagronen (Alpine Macaroni)

Älplermagronen is a classic Swiss comfort food, often referred to as Alpine macaroni. It combines macaroni with potatoes, Swiss cheese (such as Gruyère), cream, and onions, creating a rich, hearty dish that's perfect for cold mountain nights.

Taste
The taste is creamy, cheesy, and slightly savory, with the earthy flavor of the potatoes and onions adding depth. The combination of cheese and cream creates a comforting texture.

Preparation
Macaroni and potatoes are boiled together, then mixed with cream and cheese. The dish is usually topped with crispy, caramelized onions for added flavor.

Where to Try

Restaurant Älplermagronen (Zermatt): Offering an authentic Alpine-style version of this dish.

Gasthof Sternen (Lucerne): A family-friendly spot with hearty Älplermagronen.

Swiss Alps: Many mountain huts offer this dish during hiking or ski season.

What Makes it Iconic?

Älplermagronen is a rustic, comforting meal that reflects the simplicity and hearty nature of Swiss mountain life. It's ideal after a day of physical activity like hiking or skiing.

Tips for Enjoying

Pair with a light salad to balance out the richness.

It's often served with apple sauce on the side—this helps cut the richness of the cheese and cream.

When making it at home, use good-quality Swiss cheese for the best flavor.

4. Swiss Chocolate

Switzerland is world-renowned for its chocolate, which has been perfected over centuries. Swiss chocolate is often made with fine cocoa beans and has a smooth, creamy texture.

Taste

The taste of Swiss chocolate is creamy, rich, and often less sweet compared to chocolates from other countries, allowing the chocolate's natural cocoa flavor to shine. The chocolate comes in various types, from milk to dark and with different flavor combinations such as hazelnuts, fruits, and spices.

Preparation

Swiss chocolate is traditionally made from cocoa beans that are roasted, ground into cocoa mass, mixed with milk and sugar, and then tempered to give it that signature smooth texture.

Where to Try

Chocolatier Läderach (Zurich): Known for its high-quality chocolates and pralines.

Maison Cailler (Broc): One of Switzerland's oldest chocolate makers where you can tour and taste.

Confiserie Bachmann (Lucerne): Offers a wide selection of local Swiss chocolates.

What Makes it Iconic?

Swiss chocolate is iconic because of its high standards in quality and its rich history. Swiss chocolatiers have been pioneers in chocolate-making innovations such as the conching process, which gives Swiss chocolate its unique smooth texture.

Tips for Enjoying

Taste the chocolate slowly to enjoy the texture and flavor notes.

Opt for high-quality dark chocolate, which offers a more intense cocoa flavor.

If visiting a chocolatier, ask for a tasting experience to learn more about the chocolate-making process.

5. Zürcher Geschnetzeltes (Zurich-style Veal)

This dish is a specialty of Zurich, consisting of veal sliced into thin strips and cooked in a creamy white wine and mushroom sauce. It's typically served with Rösti, a Swiss-style potato dish.

Taste
The veal is tender and flavorful, and the creamy sauce, made with white wine, mushrooms, and cream, adds a rich and savory depth to the dish.

Preparation
The veal is sautéed and then simmered with white wine, cream, and mushrooms until tender. It's often served with Rösti or sometimes mashed potatoes.

Where to Try

Restaurant Zeughauskeller (Zurich): A traditional spot to try Zürcher Geschnetzeltes.

Restaurant Löwen (Zurich): A cozy, classic Zurich restaurant where this dish is a specialty.

Kronenhalle (Zurich): A fine dining institution in Zurich offering an elegant version of this dish.

What Makes it Iconic?

Zürcher Geschnetzeltes is iconic because it's a dish that represents the culinary traditions of Zurich, combining local ingredients with Swiss techniques. It's a refined yet hearty dish that's perfect for a cozy dinner.

Tips for Enjoying

Be sure to enjoy it with Rösti, as the crispy potatoes provide a perfect contrast to the creamy sauce.

This dish pairs wonderfully with a dry white Swiss wine like Chasselas.

Must-Try Dishes: Fondue, Rösti, Raclette, and More

1. Fondue

Fondue is perhaps the most iconic Swiss dish. A social meal, it involves dipping cubes of crusty bread into a pot of melted cheese. Traditionally made with a blend of **Gruyère** and **Emmental**, it's cooked with white wine and a dash of kirsch (cherry brandy) for flavor.

Types of Fondue:

Cheese Fondue: The classic version, served in a communal pot.

Fondue Bourguignonne: Meat fondue, where pieces of beef or pork are cooked in hot oil and dipped in sauces.

Chocolate Fondue: A sweet version made with melted chocolate, perfect for dipping fruits, marshmallows, and other treats.

Where to Try It: The alpine resorts of **Zermatt**, **Grindelwald**, and **Lucerne** are famous for their fondue traditions. Many mountain huts and restaurants serve fondue in the most picturesque settings.

2. Rösti

Rösti is Switzerland's answer to hash browns, but with a twist! Originating from the German-speaking part of the country, this simple yet delicious dish is made from grated potatoes, fried until crispy and golden.

Serving Styles:

Traditional: Rösti is often eaten for breakfast or as a side dish, sometimes served with eggs, bacon, or smoked salmon.

Variations: Some regions top their Rösti with cheese, onions, or even sausages.

Where to Try It: **Zurich** and the **German-speaking region** are known for Rösti, and it pairs beautifully with Swiss sausages.

3. Raclette

Another cheese dish that has become a favorite around the world, **Raclette** is both the name of the cheese and the dish. The cheese is melted and scraped onto boiled potatoes, pickled onions, and gherkins. It's a comforting dish often enjoyed in the colder months.

How It's Made: Traditionally, a large wheel of Raclette cheese is melted in front of a fire, and the molten cheese is scraped off onto the plate. Modern variations use tabletop Raclette grills to melt the cheese at the table.

Where to Try It: The **Valais region** is famous for its Raclette, and you can enjoy it in the charming Alpine towns.

4. Zürcher Geschnetzeltes

This is a Zurich specialty: **Zürcher Geschnetzeltes** is a creamy veal dish served with Rösti. The veal is sliced thinly and cooked with white wine, cream, and broth, often flavored with fresh herbs.

Where to Try It: As the name suggests, this dish is best enjoyed in **Zurich**, where it's a staple of traditional Swiss dining.

5. Saffron Risotto

While risotto is more commonly associated with Italy, **Swiss Saffron Risotto** is a local favorite, especially in the Italian-speaking region of **Ticino**. The dish is made with creamy rice and flavored with local saffron, creating a bright, aromatic dish that's often paired with fish or poultry.

Where to Try It: **Lugano** and **Ticino** offer the best versions of this Italian-influenced dish.

Swiss Chocolate and Cheese

Switzerland is globally celebrated for both its **chocolate** and **cheese**, and no trip would be complete without sampling these exceptional products.

Swiss Chocolate

Switzerland's chocolate legacy is legendary, with the country being home to some of the world's most famous chocolate brands like **Lindt**, **Toblerone**, and **Cailler**. The Swiss are known for their high-quality cocoa beans, precise manufacturing techniques, and luxurious flavors.

Popular Types of Swiss Chocolate:

Milk Chocolate: Swiss milk chocolate is creamy and rich, often blended with hazelnuts or almonds for added texture.

Dark Chocolate: The country is also known for its exceptional dark chocolate, which has a high cocoa content and intense flavor.

Truffles & Pralines: Swiss chocolatiers excel at making decadent truffles and pralines, filled with everything from ganache to fruit and nut pastes.

Toblerone: A unique triangular-shaped chocolate bar, often filled with honey and almond nougat.

Where to Try It:

Zurich: The **Lindt Chocolate Shop** is a must-visit for chocolate lovers.

Broc: Home of the **Cailler Chocolate Factory**, where you can learn about the history of Swiss chocolate and enjoy tastings.

Swiss Chocolate Tasting Tips:

Savor chocolate slowly to experience the complex flavors.

Try chocolate with different cocoa percentages (e.g., 70% dark chocolate) for a more intense taste.

Swiss Cheese

Switzerland is a cheese lover's paradise, with its distinct cheeses crafted from the lush Alpine pastures. The **Swiss Alps** provide the ideal conditions for dairy farming, resulting in rich, flavorful cheeses.

Types of Swiss Cheese:

Gruyère: A hard, nutty cheese, Gruyère is the main cheese used in fondue. It's also delicious on its own or in a sandwich.

Emmental: Known for its characteristic holes, this mild, slightly tangy cheese is a classic for Swiss fondue and also served on charcuterie boards.

Appenzeller: A slightly spicy, hard cheese with a rich flavor, often enjoyed with fruits and nuts.

Raclette: As mentioned earlier, this semi-soft cheese is melted and scraped over potatoes and other accompaniments.

Tête de Moine: A soft cheese with a unique texture, it is traditionally shaved into delicate rosettes using a special knife called a "Girolle."

Where to Try It:

Gruyères: Visit the **Gruyères region** for a taste of the eponymous cheese and a tour of the Gruyère cheese factory.

Emmental: For the perfect Emmental experience, visit the **Emmental valley**, known for its lush meadows and traditional cheese-making.

Swiss Cheese Markets: The **Zurich and Basel cheese markets** are excellent spots to sample a wide variety of local cheeses.

Travel Tip:

For an authentic culinary experience, consider visiting **cheese dairies** and **chocolate factories** across Switzerland. Many offer guided tours, tastings, and even the opportunity to create your own chocolate or cheese.

Wine Regions and Vineyards

Though often overshadowed by France and Italy, Switzerland produces exceptional wines, most of which are consumed domestically. With over 15,000 hectares of vineyards, the country boasts diverse grape varieties, stunning terroirs, and centuries of wine-making tradition.

1. Valais

Largest wine region, located in southern Switzerland along the Rhône River. Known for sunny slopes and alpine terroir.

Key Grapes: Fendant (Chasselas), Petite Arvine, Heida, Cornalin, Humagne Rouge

Highlights:

Sion and Sierre – Wine trails, cellar tours

Salgesch and Vétroz – Home to prestigious vintners

Wine festivals – Especially in autumn, featuring vineyard hikes

2. Vaud

Located on the northern shores of **Lake Geneva**, Vaud is home to the UNESCO-listed **Lavaux Vineyards**—terraced slopes with lake views.

Key Grapes: Chasselas (crisp, light white wine), Pinot Noir

Highlights:

Lavaux – Walk or bike between vineyard villages like Cully and Epesses

La Côte – Near Nyon and Rolle, known for elegant whites

Wine cellars in Montreux and Vevey

3. Geneva

One of the most productive wine areas per capita. Close to the French border, Geneva's wines often reflect a blend of Swiss and French winemaking styles.

Key Grapes: Gamay, Pinot Noir, Aligoté, Chardonnay

Highlights:

Visit local **caves (wineries)** for tastings

Annual **Fête de la Vigne et du Vin** in May

4. Ticino

The Italian-speaking canton is known for its **Merlot wines**, which are rich, structured, and pair well with hearty local cuisine.

Key Grapes: Merlot, Bondola

Highlights:

Vineyards around **Lugano, Mendrisio, and Locarno**

Food-and-wine pairings at grotti (rustic Ticino taverns)

5. German-Speaking Switzerland (Deutschschweiz)

Less known internationally but growing in reputation, especially for crisp whites and aromatic reds.

Regions: Zurich, Aargau, Schaffhausen

Key Grapes: Müller-Thurgau, Pinot Noir (Blauburgunder)

Highlights:

Rhine Valley wine walks

Boutique wineries with small production

Best Restaurants by Region

Switzerland's dining scene is as diverse as its culture—blending French finesse, Italian warmth, and German heartiness. Below are regional standouts that blend cuisine, atmosphere, and local flavor.

Zurich

Kronenhalle – Historic institution serving Swiss classics; famed for art-filled interiors

Restaurant Pavillon (Baur au Lac) – Michelin-starred French haute cuisine

Haus Hiltl – World's oldest vegetarian restaurant; modern and creative dishes

Geneva

Domaine de Châteauvieux – Two Michelin stars; elegant countryside dining with wine pairing

Bayview by Michel Roth – Lakefront, Michelin-starred, refined French-Swiss fusion

Café du Soleil – One of the best places in Geneva for traditional fondue

Lucerne

Restaurant Galerie (Hotel Montana) – Panoramic views and Mediterranean flair

Old Swiss House – Famous for schnitzel and historic Swiss décor

Mill'Feuille – Trendy bistro on the Reuss River

Bern

Kornhauskeller – Magnificent cellar restaurant with Swiss and Mediterranean dishes

Rosengarten – Scenic views of Bern's old town with excellent modern cuisine

Metzgerstübli – Local meats and traditional Bernese fare

Lausanne

Anne-Sophie Pic (Beau-Rivage Palace) – Michelin-starred, refined French elegance

Café de Grancy – Lively atmosphere, seasonal and creative Swiss food

Le Chalet Suisse – Ideal for fondue in a classic setting

Basel

Cheval Blanc by Peter Knogl – 3 Michelin stars; gourmet French cuisine

Volkshaus Basel – Stylish brasserie with a modern twist

Walliser Kanne – Cozy, traditional dishes like raclette and rösti

Zermatt

After Seven – Gourmet cuisine with artistic presentation; one Michelin star

Chez Vrony – Famous mountain restaurant; alpine gourmet with organic ingredients

Restaurant Schäferstube – Rustic, with excellent meat and cheese dishes

Interlaken & Jungfrau Region

La Terrasse (Victoria-Jungfrau Grand Hotel) – Fine dining with mountain views

Schuh Restaurant – Elegant, Swiss and French fusion with an in-house chocolatier

Bergrestaurant Allmend – Cozy mountain hut fare near Grindelwald

Lugano (Ticino)

Grotto della Salute – Rustic Ticinese dishes under chestnut trees

Arte al Lago – Michelin-starred lakeside dining with Mediterranean influence

Grotto Morchino – Family-run, charming, traditional southern Swiss cuisine

Travel Tip:

Switzerland's best wine and dining experiences often come from local or family-run establishments. Book reservations early, especially for Michelin-starred restaurants, and ask locals for current seasonal favorites.

Chapter 11: 7-Day Ultimate Switzerland Adventure

Day 1: Arrival in Zurich & Explore the City

Morning

Arrival at Zurich Airport (ZRH)

Transport to City: Take the **S-Bahn (S2 or S16)** or **train to Zürich HB (Main Station)** – 10-15 minutes.

Cost: CHF 6.80 (2nd class)

Getting Around: Use the **Zurich Card** (CHF 27 for 24 hours) for unlimited travel on public transport and discounts on museums.

Check-in at your hotel or drop luggage if too early. Recommended central areas to stay: **Old Town (Altstadt)** or near **Bahnhofstrasse**.

Breakfast:

Café Sprüngli (Paradeplatz)

Try: Birchermüesli (Swiss-style muesli), Zopf bread with butter and jam, and a cappuccino.

Cost: CHF 15–20

Hours: 7:00 AM – 6:30 PM

Mid-Morning

Bahnhofstrasse Walk & Window Shopping

One of the world's most exclusive shopping streets.

Optional: Visit **Confiserie Teuscher** for handmade Swiss chocolate.

Visit Lindenhof Hill

A peaceful viewpoint overlooking the Old Town and Limmat River.

Free entry, open 24/7.

Switzerland Travel Guide 2025`

Afternoon

Lunch:

Restaurant Zeughauskeller (Swiss-German fare in a former armory)

Try: Zürcher Geschnetzeltes (veal in cream sauce with Rösti)

Cost: CHF 25–35

Hours: 11:30 AM – 11:00 PM

Explore Old Town (Altstadt)

Walk through narrow medieval alleys, boutiques, bookstores.

Visit **Grossmünster Church** (iconic twin towers)

Hours: 10:00 AM – 6:00 PM

Cost: Free (CHF 5 to climb tower)

Mid-Afternoon

Visit Kunsthaus Zürich (Zurich Art Museum)

World-class collection from Swiss and European masters

Hours: 10:00 AM – 6:00 PM (Thurs until 8 PM)

Cost: CHF 23 (free with Zurich Card)

OR

Take a 1-hour Lake Zurich Cruise from Bürkliplatz

Cost: CHF 8.80 with Zurich Card`

Departure every hour, last one around 5:30 PM

Evening

Dinner:

Swiss Chuchi (Hotel Adler) for traditional Swiss cuisine

Try: Cheese fondue or Raclette

Cost: CHF 30–40

Hours: 11:30 AM – 10:00 PM

Night Stroll:

Walk along the **Limmatquai**, enjoy the lights on the water.

Stop by **Bar am Wasser** (for a nightcap) near Storchen Zurich.

Drink Cost: CHF 12–18

Day 2: Day Trip to Lucerne

Morning

Travel to Lucerne by Train

From Zurich HB to Lucerne station

Duration: ~50 minutes (trains every 30 min)

Cost: CHF 15–25 one way with Half Fare Card

Depart early (~7:30 AM) to maximize the day.

Breakfast in Lucerne:

Heini Conditorei (near station)

Try: Croissants, espresso, local pastries like Nidelkuchen

Cost: CHF 10–15

Hours: 6:30 AM – 6:30 PM

Mid-Morning

Explore Old Town (Altstadt)

Colorful facades, fountains, frescoes

Walk across **Chapel Bridge (Kapellbrücke)**

Visit **Jesuit Church** (free, open 8 AM – 6:30 PM)

Optional: Museum Sammlung Rosengart

Switzerland Travel Guide 2025`

Picasso and Klee collections

Hours: 10:00 AM – 6:00 PM

Cost: CHF 18

Afternoon

Lunch:

Wirtshaus Galliker (classic Swiss tavern)

Try: Luzerner Chügelipastete (veal-filled puff pastry)

Cost: CHF 25–35

Hours: 11:30 AM – 2:00 PM, 6:00 PM – 10:00 PM

Visit the Lion Monument (Löwendenkmal)

Iconic sculpture commemorating Swiss Guards

Free, open 24/7

Nearby **Glacier Garden** (Gletschergarten)

Cost: CHF 22

Hours: 10:00 AM – 6:00 PM

Mid-Afternoon

Ride the Lucerne–Lake Lucerne Boat Cruise

1-hour panoramic cruise

Cost: CHF 25 (covered by Swiss Travel Pass)

Departs: Near Bahnhofquai, hourly from noon

OR

Take the City Wall Walk (Museggmauer)

Open: April–November

Climb towers for views of the city

Free entry, open until 7 PM

Evening

Dinner before returning to Zurich:

Restaurant Fritschi

Try: Rösti variations, local fish dishes

Cost: CHF 30–40

Hours: 11:00 AM – 11:00 PM

Return Train to Zurich

Trains run until late night (e.g., 8:30 PM, 9:30 PM, etc.)

Back to hotel by 10:00–10:30 PM

Travel Tips

Zurich Card: Ideal for Day 1 (CHF 27/day).

Swiss Half Fare Card: CHF 120 for one month, cuts all transport and mountain trip costs in half.

Swiss Travel Pass: CHF 232 for 3 days, covers all trains, boats, and many museums.

Download **SBB Mobile App** for schedules, prices, and tickets.

Switzerland Travel Guide 2025`

Day 3: Travel to Interlaken & Adventure Activities

Morning

Travel from Zurich to Interlaken

Route: Zurich HB → Bern → Interlaken Ost

Duration: ~2 hours

Cost: CHF 34–60 (50% off with Swiss Half Fare Card)

Depart early (~7:00 AM) to reach by 9:30 AM

Breakfast in Zurich before departure:

Babu's Bakery & Coffeehouse

Try: Avocado toast, eggs, fresh juice

Cost: CHF 15–20

Hours: 7:30 AM – 6:00 PM

Check in or drop off luggage at hotel in Interlaken (recommend staying near **Interlaken Ost or West station**)

Mid-Morning

Orientation Walk in Interlaken

Stroll along **Höhematte Park** for views of paragliders and the surrounding Alps.

Visit **Kirchhofer Swiss Watch Store** or local chocolate shops.

Afternoon

Lunch:

Hüsi Bierhaus (craft beer and hearty fare)

Try: Swiss sausages, Rösti

Cost: CHF 20–30

Hours: 11:00 AM – late

Adventure Activity Options (choose one):

Paragliding over Interlaken

Time: 1.5–2 hours including transport

Cost: ~CHF 170

Booking: *Paragliding Interlaken*

Canyoning (Beginner level)

Time: ~3 hours

Cost: CHF 130

Available: Spring–early Autumn

Harder Kulm Funicular

Panoramic views over Interlaken and Lakes Thun & Brienz

Cost: CHF 38 return (CHF 19 with Half Fare Card)

Hours: 9:10 AM – 9:10 PM

Restaurant at the top for optional drinks/snack

Mid-Afternoon

Relax at Lake Brienz or Lake Thun

Rent a paddle boat or take a lakeside stroll.

Optional boat cruise: CHF 30 (covered by Swiss Travel Pass)

Evening

Dinner:

Restaurant Taverne (Hotel Interlaken)

Try: Grilled trout or traditional fondue

Cost: CHF 30–40

Hours: 6:00 PM – 10:00 PM

Night

Relax at the hotel or stroll through Interlaken West's shopping street.

Optional: Try **Casino Interlaken** (entry CHF 10, passport required)

Day 4: Jungfraujoch – Top of Europe

Morning

Early Departure from Interlaken Ost to Jungfraujoch

Route: Interlaken Ost → Lauterbrunnen/Grindelwald → Kleine Scheidegg → Jungfraujoch

Duration: ~2.5 hours one way

First train: ~6:35 AM

Cost: CHF 100–120 with Half Fare Card (CHF 210 full price)

Book in advance for best weather & seat reservations

Breakfast:

Grab a quick bite from **Backerei Konditorei Café Mohler** (near Interlaken Ost)

Try: Coffee, sandwich, fruit tart

Cost: CHF 10–15

Hours: From 6:00 AM

Mid-Morning to Afternoon

Explore Jungfraujoch (Top of Europe)

Alpine Sensation Walk, Ice Palace, Observation Deck, and **Plateau Snow Fun Zone**

Eat at: Restaurant **Bollywood** or **Top of Europe Self Service**

Try: Swiss Indian fusion or simple alpine dishes

Cost: CHF 25–35

Plan to depart around 2:00–3:00 PM to avoid late afternoon crowds.

Mid-Afternoon

Stop at Kleine Scheidegg or Wengen on your return for a coffee with a view.

Wengen is car-free, peaceful, and charming.

Evening

Back in Interlaken by 5:00–6:00 PM

Dinner:

Ox Restaurant & Grill

Try: Burgers, local beef dishes, vegetarian options

Cost: CHF 25–35

Hours: 6:00 PM – 10:30 PM

Night

Chill at the hotel or enjoy a late walk under the mountain stars.

Day 5: Zermatt & Matterhorn Views

Morning

Early train from Interlaken Ost to Zermatt

Route: Interlaken → Spiez → Visp → Zermatt

Duration: ~2.5 hours

Cost: CHF 60–90 (50% off with Half Fare Card)

Depart by 7:00 AM

Breakfast on the train or grab something from **Migros Takeaway** before departure.

Mid-Morning

Arrival in car-free Zermatt

Walk or take an **electro-taxi** to hotel to drop luggage.

Explore Zermatt Village:

Bahnhofstrasse boutiques, chocolate shops, and Matterhorn Museum (CHF 10, open 11:00 AM – 6:00 PM)

Afternoon

Lunch:

Restaurant Whymper-Stube

Try: Cheese fondue, Valais specialties

Cost: CHF 30–40

Hours: 11:30 AM – 9:30 PM

Visit Matterhorn Glacier Paradise (Klein Matterhorn)

Europe's highest cable car station

Panoramic views, ice palace, snow year-round

Cost: CHF 90 return (CHF 45 with Half Fare Card)

Cable car hours: 8:30 AM – 4:00 PM (last return ~4:30 PM)

Ride time: ~45 mins one way

OR

Gornergrat Bahn (Cogwheel Train)

Stunning Matterhorn panorama

Cost: CHF 88 return (CHF 44 with Half Fare Card)

Ride time: 33 minutes

Hours: 7:00 AM – 6:30 PM

Mid-Afternoon

Hot chocolate or snack at Findlerhof (requires short hike or funicular + walk)

Unmatched Matterhorn views and charming alpine vibe

Evening

Dinner:

Restaurant Schäferstube

Try: Lamb dishes, Rösti, Raclette

Cost: CHF 30–45

Hours: 6:00 PM – 10:00 PM

Night

Stroll under the lit-up Matterhorn (weather permitting)

Optionally stay overnight in Zermatt or return to Interlaken (if tight on time)

Day 6: Glacier Express & Chur

Morning

Breakfast at your hotel in Zermatt

Board the Glacier Express to Chur

Departs: ~8:52 AM (subject to seasonal schedule)

Duration: ~8 hours

Reservation mandatory

Cost:

Ticket: CHF ~150 (CHF 75 with Half Fare Card)

Reservation: CHF 39–49 depending on class/season

What to Expect: Panoramic windows, slow scenic journey through Alps, 291 bridges, 91 tunnels

Lunch onboard:

3-course menu available

Cost: CHF 35–45

Must pre-book or order early during the trip

Afternoon

Continue enjoying the scenic ride

Highlights: Oberalp Pass (2,033 m), Rhine Gorge (Swiss Grand Canyon)

Arrive in Chur around 5:00–6:00 PM

Explore Chur Old Town briefly (if time allows)

Alternatively, take an evening train to **Zurich** (1.5 hours)

Train Chur to Zurich

Trains every hour

Cost: CHF 24–48 (CHF 12–24 with Half Fare Card)

Evening

Dinner in Zurich (if staying overnight):

Raclette Stube – traditional Swiss melted cheese dishes

Try: Raclette with pickles, potatoes, and onions

Cost: CHF 30–40

Hours: 6:00 PM – 10:00 PM

Check-in at Zurich hotel (recommend near Zurich HB for convenience)

Switzerland Travel Guide 2025`

Day 7: Departure from Zurich

Morning

Breakfast at hotel or at the station (Brezelkönig or Coop Pronto for take-away)

Try: Fresh pretzel sandwich and coffee

Cost: CHF 5–10

Transfer to Zurich Airport (ZRH)

Train from Zurich HB: every 5–10 minutes

Duration: ~10–15 minutes

Cost: CHF 6.80 (CHF 3.40 with Half Fare Card)

Tips:

Arrive at the airport at least 2 hours before your flight

Luggage lockers are available at Zurich HB if you have time before heading out

Chapter 12: Sustainable and Responsible Travel

Eco-Friendly Transportation

Switzerland is a global leader in sustainable mobility, offering tourists multiple ways to explore the country with minimal environmental impact.

1. Swiss Public Transportation: Efficient and Green

Trains, buses, and boats are powered increasingly by renewable energy—especially hydropower.

The **Swiss Federal Railways (SBB)** boasts one of the most eco-friendly train networks in Europe.

PostBuses (PostAuto) connect even remote alpine villages with low-emission vehicles.

Why it's green:

Over 90% of electricity powering the Swiss rail network comes from renewable sources.

2. Scenic Trains with a Light Footprint

Trains like the **Glacier Express**, **Bernina Express**, and **GoldenPass Line** let you admire the beauty of Switzerland without leaving a carbon trail.

Tip: Use panoramic trains instead of renting cars—better for the environment and more relaxing.

3. Bike Sharing & E-Bikes

Cities like Zurich, Bern, and Geneva have extensive **bike-sharing networks** (e.g., PubliBike, Donkey Republic). Many towns offer **e-bike rentals** for mountainous terrain.

Bike paths are clearly marked, scenic, and safe.

Regional rail stations often feature integrated bike stations.

4. Walking & Hiking

The Swiss have built an extraordinary **network of 65,000+ kilometers** of marked walking and hiking trails.

National parks and nature reserves promote low-impact foot traffic.

Many hotels provide **free local transport passes** encouraging walking and public transport use.

5. Electric Car Rentals

If you must drive, opt for **electric vehicle rentals** (available from Sixt, Europcar, etc.). Charging stations are widespread, especially in cities and along major highways.

Green Hotels and Lodges

Switzerland's eco-conscious approach extends to its accommodations, from luxury resorts to mountain cabins. Many properties follow **sustainability certifications** such as:

ibex fairstay (Swiss eco-label for hotels)

Swisstainable (a national label encouraging sustainable tourism)

Green Globe and **EU Ecolabel**

1. Notable Eco-Friendly Hotels

Whitepod Eco-Luxury Hotel – Valais

Geodesic pods in the mountains with minimal environmental footprint

Uses renewable energy, local sourcing, and zero-waste practices

Hotel Gstaad Palace – Gstaad

Implements strict sustainability standards

Uses hydropower, sources regional produce, and limits plastic

Schweizerhof Hotel – Lucerne

Certified with **ibex fairstay** for long-term eco-efforts

Switzerland Travel Guide 2025`

Offers waste separation, green energy, and low-impact guest programs

Jugendherberge (Swiss Youth Hostels)

Over 50 hostels certified for their eco-friendly initiatives

Affordable, central, and perfect for budget-conscious green travelers

2. Alpine Lodges and Mountain Cabins

Many **Swiss Alpine Club (SAC)** huts and rural lodges use **solar panels**, **rainwater collection**, and **compost toilets**.

They promote "leave no trace" principles and often offer local organic meals.

3. Tips for Choosing Green Stays

Look for **"Swisstainable" Level II or III** labels when booking.

Choose properties that:

Use renewable energy

Employ local staff and buy regional goods

Promote recycling and zero-waste goals

Supporting Local Communities

Switzerland is more than just mountains and trains—its soul lies in its local communities, small producers, and age-old traditions. Supporting them ensures that tourism contributes positively to local livelihoods.

1. Stay Local

Choose family-run hotels, guesthouses, and mountain lodges over international chains.

Look for **farm stays or B&Bs** that promote traditional Swiss hospitality, such as those in the Emmental or Ticino regions.

2. Shop Locally Made Goods

Buy from local artisans instead of mass-produced souvenirs. Look for handmade watches, woodcrafts, regional textiles, or natural cosmetics.

Farmers' markets (e.g., in Lausanne, Lucerne, and Zurich) offer fresh, regional food and help support Swiss farmers directly.

3. Eat Local

Dine at **locally owned restaurants**, cafés, and alpine huts that use regional ingredients.

Try **local food specialties** from different cantons—cheese from Gruyères, wine from Valais, or dried meat from Graubünden.

4. Book Local Tours

Choose **independent guides** or small, community-based tour operators. Many offer cultural experiences, village walks, cheese-making, or wildlife tours.

Examples:

Family-run paragliding schools in Interlaken

Village cooking classes in Ticino

Guided hikes by locals in the Bernese Oberland

5. Support Cultural Events

Attend **local festivals, concerts, and folklore events**, which help sustain regional identities and traditions.

Consider making donations to **preservation groups or museums**, especially in remote villages.

Waste Management and Recycling in Switzerland

Switzerland is globally admired for its clean streets, clear lakes, and efficient recycling system. Tourists are expected to participate in these efforts as well.

1. Recycling Culture

Switzerland has one of the highest recycling rates in the world. Most towns and cities have clearly marked bins for:

PET plastic bottles

Glass (sorted by color)

Aluminum and metal

Paper and cardboard

Organic waste (compost)

2. Waste Separation in Hotels and Apartments

Most accommodations provide **separate bins** for recycling. If not, ask the front desk for guidance.

Short-term rentals (Airbnbs, chalets) often require guests to **sort and dispose of waste at designated recycling centers**—typically located nearby.

3. Bottle and Can Returns

Many supermarkets have **return stations for bottles and cans**—some offer a small refund or store credit.

Reusable glass milk bottles and **returnable beer bottles** are common.

4. Avoid Single-Use Plastics

Carry a **reusable water bottle** (tap water is safe and excellent everywhere).

Use **fabric tote bags** or **reusable shopping bags**—plastic bags are either banned or cost extra.

Refuse disposable cutlery and packaging when buying take-out meals.

5. Trash Disposal Rules

In many municipalities, trash can only be disposed of in **officially designated bags (e.g., "Züri-Sack" in Zurich)**, which must be purchased. This system incentivizes recycling and reduces landfill waste.

Quick Tips for Responsible Travelers:

Learn local **waste disposal rules** in the region you're visiting.

When hiking, **pack out everything**—leave no waste behind in nature.

Respect **quiet hours and public cleanliness standards**, especially in villages.

Ask locals how you can support their businesses or events—most are happy to share.

Ethical Outdoor Practices

Switzerland's mountains, forests, lakes, and meadows are world-famous—and incredibly fragile. Ethical outdoor behavior preserves these spaces for future generations and respects local wildlife, ecosystems, and communities.

1. Stay on Marked Trails

Switzerland has over **65,000 km of marked hiking and walking paths**. Stick to these to avoid trampling sensitive flora or disturbing protected zones.

Venturing off-trail can contribute to **soil erosion**, damage alpine vegetation, or disrupt farming lands.

2. Respect Wildlife

Observe animals from a distance. **Never feed, chase, or attempt to pet wild animals**, even marmots or ibexes that may seem used to humans.

In national parks and reserves, **quiet observation** is key—binoculars or zoom lenses are great tools for ethical wildlife watching.

3. Leave No Trace

Pack out all waste, including food wrappers, tissues, and biodegradable waste like fruit peels.

If there's no trash bin nearby, carry a small garbage bag and dispose of it properly when you return to town.

Toilet use: In remote areas, bury human waste far from trails or water sources, or use eco-toilets if available.

4. Respect Quiet Zones and Other People

In rural or alpine settings, sound carries far. **Avoid loud music, shouting, or drone usage** that could disturb wildlife or fellow hikers.

Yield to uphill hikers and greet fellow travelers with a polite "Grüezi" or "Bonjour," depending on the region.

5. Camp Responsibly (Or Not at All)

Wild camping is not widely allowed in Switzerland, especially in protected areas. Always check cantonal regulations.

Use **designated campgrounds or mountain huts** (e.g., Swiss Alpine Club huts), which are managed sustainably.

If permitted to camp, **set up after dusk and pack up by dawn**, and **leave the site exactly as you found it**.

6. Mind Local Agriculture and Pastures

Many trails cross **private farmland or alpine pastures**. Always **close gates, don't touch fences**, and **keep a respectful distance from grazing animals**.

If hiking with a dog, **keep it leashed**—especially near livestock or wildlife zones.

7. Fire Safety and Cooking

Open fires are banned in many areas due to wildfire risks. Use **designated fire pits** where allowed.

Avoid leaving any burned materials or ashes behind. In high-risk seasons, **use portable stoves** instead.

8. Support Preservation Efforts

Consider donating to or volunteering with local conservation groups or national parks.

Follow ranger guidelines, local signs, and park-specific rules, which may vary by region or season.

Extra: Ethical Winter Sports Behavior

Stay within **marked ski and snowboard zones**—going off-piste can damage habitats or cause avalanches.

Do not disturb hibernating wildlife, such as in snowy forests or remote slopes.

Always **carry out all trash**, including energy bar wrappers and disposable hand warmers.

Chapter 13: Shopping in Switzerland

Swiss Watches and Timepieces

Switzerland is the world's capital of fine watchmaking, blending heritage craftsmanship, cutting-edge innovation, and timeless design. Whether you're a collector or just want a stylish souvenir, buying a watch in Switzerland is both a personal investment and a cultural experience.

1. Why Swiss Watches Are So Renowned

Precision engineering: Known globally for exceptional accuracy and durability.

Craftsmanship: Many brands still manufacture and assemble watches by hand.

Innovation: Swiss makers lead in mechanical movements, chronographs, and hybrid smartwatches.

Prestige: Wearing a Swiss watch is often seen as a status symbol.

2. Top Swiss Watch Brands

Luxury: Rolex, Patek Philippe, Audemars Piguet, Vacheron Constantin

Mid-range: TAG Heuer, Longines, Omega, Tissot

Entry-level and Fashion: Swatch, Mondaine (maker of the official Swiss railway watch), Victorinox

3. Where to Buy

Geneva and Zurich: Flagship stores and high-end boutiques (e.g., Bucherer, Les Ambassadeurs)

Factory outlets: Some towns like **Biel/Bienne** (watchmaking capital) have direct factory outlets offering better deals.

Authorized retailers: Always buy from official dealers to ensure authenticity and warranties.

4. Tips for Buying a Watch

Know your **budget** and preferred **style** (mechanical vs quartz, sport vs dress).

Ask about **tax-free shopping**—tourists can reclaim VAT on departure.

Request an **international warranty** and **certificate of authenticity**.

Be wary of counterfeit goods, especially from unauthorized street vendors.

Chocolate, Cheese, and Gourmet Gifts

Switzerland offers a culinary paradise for lovers of fine food, with chocolates and cheeses that are as culturally rich as they are delicious.

1. Swiss Chocolate

Renowned for its **creaminess and purity**, Swiss chocolate is a must-buy gift or indulgence.

Top Brands: Lindt, Läderach, Sprüngli, Cailler (Nestlé-owned), and Villars.

Artisan Chocolatiers: Try handcrafted varieties from Max Chocolatier (Lucerne), Du Rhône (Geneva), or Confiserie Bachmann (Zurich).

What to Buy:

Pralines and truffles

Chocolate bars with Alpine ingredients (hazelnuts, berries)

Hot chocolate blends

Chocolate gift boxes in traditional packaging

Tip: Many stores offer on-site tastings and allow you to create custom assortments.

2. Swiss Cheese

Switzerland produces over **450 varieties of cheese**, most made in small batches using traditional methods.

Must-Try Varieties:

Gruyère: Nutty, semi-hard cheese used in fondue

Emmental: Classic "Swiss cheese" with holes

Appenzeller: Strong flavor, aged in herbal brine

Tête de Moine: Served in delicate rosettes using a special tool called a girolle

Where to Buy:

Specialty cheese shops

Supermarkets (Migros, Coop) carry excellent local options

Cheese dairies and farm stores in regions like Gruyères, Emmental, and Appenzell

Tip: Many cheese shops vacuum-seal products for air travel.

3. Other Gourmet Swiss Gifts

Honey and Alpine herbs from mountain regions

Local jams made with berries from Valais or Graubünden

Sausages and dried meats like Bündnerfleisch (Graubünden)

Swiss herbal teas and natural infusions

Regional wines and spirits, especially white wines from Valais or kirsch (cherry brandy)

Final Tips:

Combine purchases for **VAT refunds** (minimum purchase amount usually CHF 300 per store).

Customs regulations: Check duty-free limits for food or alcohol before flying home.

Choose **eco-packaged or locally sourced gifts** to support sustainable producers.

Local Artisans and Craft Markets

Switzerland has a strong heritage of fine craftsmanship rooted in centuries of Alpine culture. From woodcarving to handmade textiles, travelers seeking authentic and meaningful souvenirs will find a wealth of options in artisan shops and regional markets.

1. What You'll Find

Woodcarvings: Especially in areas like Brienz, famous for intricate figurines and nativity sets.

Textiles and Embroidery: Traditional table linens, lacework, and handwoven fabrics from Appenzell and St. Gallen.

Ceramics and Pottery: Hand-painted earthenware and stoneware from rural studios.

Paper Art and Scherenschnitt: Intricate silhouette paper cuttings, common in Bernese Oberland and Emmental.

Handcrafted Jewelry: Often made with local gemstones or Alpine motifs.

Alpine Bells (Trycheln): Beautifully decorated cowbells, a symbol of Swiss heritage.

Natural Body Products: Handmade soaps, salves, and perfumes using Alpine herbs and essential oils.

2. Where to Shop

Weekly and seasonal markets:

Bern's weekly market (Bundesplatz)

Zurich's Bürkliplatz market (Tuesdays and Fridays)

Montreux and Lucerne Christmas Markets

Local craft fairs: Especially active during holidays and harvest seasons.

Village artisan shops: In places like Appenzell, Gruyères, and Lauterbrunnen.

Alpine museums and workshops: Some offer hands-on experiences, like cheese-making or woodcarving.

3. Shopping Tips

Look for **"Handgemacht"** (handmade) labels or certification from local artisan associations.

Ask about the **artist's story**—many vendors are happy to explain their heritage and process.

Buy **early in the day** at markets for the best selection and least crowding.

High-End Boutiques and Luxury Goods

On the other end of the spectrum, Switzerland is a paradise for luxury shopping—particularly for those looking to invest in fashion, jewelry, and designer goods with Swiss precision and European flair.

1. What's Available

Luxury Watches & Jewelry: Rolex, Omega, Chopard, and Cartier are widely available, especially in Geneva and Zurich.

Designer Fashion: International brands like Chanel, Hermès, Louis Vuitton, and Swiss designers such as Akris.

Fine Leather Goods: Handcrafted bags, gloves, and wallets, often made in small ateliers.

Perfumes and Beauty Products: Swiss skincare brands like La Prairie and Valmont offer high-end beauty treatments.

Home Décor & Crystal: Elegant tableware, crystal, and art glass from brands like Baccarat and Lalique (often sold in Swiss boutiques).

2. Where to Shop

Bahnhofstrasse, Zurich: One of the world's most prestigious shopping streets, lined with luxury flagships.

Rue du Rhône, Geneva: Ideal for luxury watches, jewelry, and designer fashion.

Gstaad & St. Moritz: Exclusive resort towns known for high-end boutiques and private shopping experiences.

Luxury department stores:

Globus (Zurich, Geneva, Lausanne)

Jelmoli (Zurich's largest premium department store)

3. Shopping Tips

Ask about **VAT refunds**—non-EU tourists can claim back a portion of taxes with eligible purchases.

Bring your passport when making luxury purchases to process tax-free forms on the spot.

Swiss sales staff are discreet and knowledgeable—don't hesitate to ask for **custom fittings, packaging, or international delivery**.

VAT Refund and Shopping Tips

Switzerland is known for premium-quality products—from watches to cheese—but shopping smartly can help you save significantly. As a tourist, you're entitled to reclaim Value Added Tax (VAT) on eligible purchases.

1. VAT Refund: What You Need to Know

Swiss VAT (Mehrwertsteuer) is currently **7.7%** on most goods and services.

Tourists from **non-EU countries** are eligible for refunds on goods exported within **30 days** of purchase.

2. Minimum Spend & Requirements

The **minimum purchase per receipt** to qualify for VAT refund is **CHF 300** (including VAT) at one store, on the same day.

Goods must be **unused** and taken out of Switzerland in personal luggage.

You need to **present your passport** when making the purchase.

3. How to Claim Your Refund

At the store: Ask for a **Tax-Free Form** when you make a qualifying purchase.

At the airport or border: Have your goods, receipts, and forms **ready for inspection** by Swiss Customs before check-in.

Once stamped, submit your forms at a **VAT refund office** (like Global Blue or Planet) for a **cash refund or card credit**. You can also mail it in later.

Tip: Allow extra time at the airport for VAT processing—queues can be long at major hubs like Zurich and Geneva.

4. Practical Shopping Tips

Check return policies, especially when purchasing high-value goods.

Compare prices between stores—especially for luxury items or electronics.

Keep all **receipts and packaging** until you leave the country.

Chapter 14: Practical Information and Travel Tips

Currency, Banking, and Credit Cards

Switzerland uses the **Swiss Franc (CHF)** as its official currency, and understanding how to manage your finances while traveling can make your trip smoother.

1. Currency and Exchange

Swiss Franc (CHF): The official currency, often abbreviated as CHF or written as "Fr." or "SFr."

Exchange Rates: Switzerland is not part of the European Union, so the **Euro** is not widely accepted (although some tourist areas might accept it, expect to pay a premium). Always check exchange rates before exchanging money at banks or exchange offices.

ATMs: Swiss ATMs are widely available, and you can withdraw CHF using international credit or debit cards. Be mindful of **foreign transaction fees** your bank may charge.

Currency Exchange Services: You can find exchange services at major airports, train stations, and some hotels. **Avoid exchanging currency at airports** if possible, as they often offer less favorable rates.

2. Banking and Cash Withdrawals

Opening a Bank Account: For short-term stays, opening a bank account is not necessary unless you're planning to reside in Switzerland. ATMs provide easy access to cash, which is the most commonly used payment method.

Bank Hours: Banks are typically open Monday to Friday, 8:30 AM to 12:00 PM, and 1:30 PM to 5:00 PM. Some banks in major cities stay open during lunch hours, while others are closed in the afternoon.

Bank Cards: Most major international bank cards (Visa, Mastercard, American Express) are accepted in Switzerland. However, always **inform your bank about your travel dates** to avoid your card being flagged for suspicious activity.

3. Credit Cards and Contactless Payments

Credit Cards: Widely accepted at hotels, restaurants, and shops. However, some smaller shops or rural areas may only accept **Swiss Francs in cash**, so always have some CHF on hand.

Contactless Payments: **Apple Pay, Google Pay, and contactless credit cards** are commonly accepted in Switzerland. In many places, **tap-and-go** is the preferred method of payment.

4. Tipping in Switzerland

Service charge: A service charge is typically included in your bill, but it's common to round up or leave a **5-10% tip** at restaurants.

Taxi: Rounding up to the nearest Franc is appreciated, but tipping is not mandatory.

Hotel: For hotel staff, leaving a small tip of **CHF 1-2** per night is customary.

Health & Safety Advice

Switzerland is known for its excellent healthcare system and safety, but there are a few things to consider to ensure a safe and healthy visit.

1. Health Insurance and Medical Care

Travel Insurance: It's **highly recommended** to have travel insurance that covers **medical emergencies, hospital stays,** and **medical evacuation** if you're traveling from outside the EU/Schengen area. Ensure it covers activities like hiking or skiing if you plan on engaging in adventure sports.

Healthcare System: Switzerland's healthcare system is one of the best in the world, but it's also expensive. Without insurance, you may face high out-of-pocket costs. **Public health services** are of excellent quality, and you'll find **pharmacies** (Apotheken) in most towns for minor ailments.

European Health Insurance Card (EHIC): If you're an EU/EEA national, carry your **EHIC** for emergency healthcare coverage in Switzerland.

2. Vaccinations and Health Precautions

General Vaccinations: No specific vaccinations are required for travelers visiting Switzerland. However, it's a good idea to be up to date on standard vaccinations like **MMR** (measles, mumps, rubella), **tetanus**, and **diphtheria**.

Altitude Sickness: If you're visiting the **Swiss Alps**, especially at higher altitudes (above 2,500 meters), take care to **acclimatize gradually**. Drink plenty of water, eat light meals, and avoid heavy exercise at high altitudes to avoid **altitude sickness**.

Insect Protection: In the warmer months, consider wearing **insect repellent** to protect against ticks, especially if hiking in rural areas or near forests, as ticks can carry diseases like Lyme disease.

3. Emergency Numbers and First Aid

Emergency Numbers: In case of an emergency, dial **112** (EU emergency number) or **144** for medical emergencies. Ambulance services are swift and highly professional.

Pharmacies: For minor illnesses or injuries, **pharmacies** are easy to find. Many pharmacies offer basic first aid supplies, over-the-counter medications, and advice.

4. Safety Tips

General Safety: Switzerland is one of the safest countries in the world, with low crime rates. However, common sense applies: keep valuables like wallets, cameras, and phones secure, particularly in crowded areas such as train stations, tourist attractions, or festivals.

Natural Hazards: If you're engaging in outdoor activities, such as hiking, skiing, or mountain climbing, **be aware of weather conditions** and follow local guidelines. The Swiss mountains, while beautiful, can be dangerous due to **avalanches** or **stormy weather**.

Wildlife: Be mindful of wild animals, particularly in rural and mountainous areas. **Bears** and **wolves** are rare but occasionally spotted, and certain areas may have **snakes** or other wildlife. Always follow local advice and signage when outdoors.

5. Personal Safety in Cities

Crime: Petty crime, such as pickpocketing, is rare but can occasionally happen in busy tourist areas or public transport. Use common sense: secure your belongings and avoid leaving them unattended.

Street Safety: Swiss cities are pedestrian-friendly with well-marked crosswalks and traffic signals. Always obey pedestrian signals and be cautious near tram or train stations.

Final Tips for a Safe Trip:

Carry **emergency contact numbers** (e.g., your country's embassy, local doctors).

Stay hydrated and well-rested, especially if you're engaging in physical activities or traveling at higher altitudes.

Carry a small first aid kit with basics like bandages, pain relief, and any prescription medications you may need.

Internet, SIM Cards, and Connectivity

Staying connected during your travels in Switzerland is easy, thanks to the country's well-developed telecommunications infrastructure. Whether you need to access the internet, make calls, or stay in touch with family and friends, here's what you need to know.

1. Internet Connectivity

Wi-Fi Access: Most hotels, cafes, restaurants, and public spaces in Switzerland offer **free Wi-Fi**. Look for the "Wi-Fi" or "Internet" sign in cafes and other public places. Some establishments may require you to register before granting access, so it's always a good idea to ask for the Wi-Fi code upon arrival.

Public Wi-Fi Networks: Large Swiss cities like Zurich, Geneva, and Bern have **free public Wi-Fi** networks in key areas such as train stations, airports, and parks. Check local websites or apps for specific locations.

2. SIM Cards for Tourists

SIM Cards for Tourists: Switzerland offers several prepaid SIM card options, allowing you to stay connected without high roaming charges.

Swisscom: Offers nationwide coverage and is one of the largest telecom providers in Switzerland. You can purchase a prepaid SIM card at any Swisscom store, major airports, or online.

Sunrise: Another popular provider offering flexible prepaid plans for data, calls, and texts. Available at Sunrise stores and some retail locations.

Salt: A good option for budget-conscious travelers with competitive prices and excellent coverage. Available in stores, including airports.

How to Buy a SIM Card:

You can purchase a SIM card directly at major **airports** (Zurich, Geneva) upon arrival, or at **mobile carrier shops**, convenience stores, and electronics retailers throughout the country.

Documents: Be sure to carry your **passport** when purchasing a SIM card, as you'll need it for registration.

Plans and Pricing:

Prepaid plans typically come with data, local calls, and international options. Expect to pay around **CHF 20-40** for a SIM card with **4GB-10GB data**.

Roaming: If you're from the EU/EEA, check if your home carrier offers **EU-wide data roaming** to use in Switzerland without incurring extra charges.

3. Mobile Data and Roaming

If you don't want to buy a local SIM, consider **roaming services**. Check with your mobile provider about roaming plans, especially for **data** usage.

Many European mobile networks now offer **EU-roaming packages**, which might also apply in Switzerland.

For travelers from outside the EU, **international roaming** can be expensive, so purchasing a Swiss SIM card is usually the better option for cost savings.

Useful Apps for Travel in Switzerland

Switzerland is a technologically advanced country, and there are plenty of apps that can enhance your travel experience—from navigation to dining recommendations, transport schedules, and cultural insights. Here are some essential apps to download for your Swiss adventure:

1. Public Transportation

SBB Mobile: The official Swiss Federal Railways (SBB) app. It provides **train schedules**, ticket purchases, and real-time travel updates. It covers **trains, buses, trams**, and other public transport across Switzerland.

ZVV Ticket: If you're traveling in Zurich, the **ZVV** app provides easy access to **ticketing, schedules**, and **real-time public transport information** for trams, buses, and trains within Zurich.

Moovit: A global transit app that provides real-time public transport schedules and routes for **buses, trams, trains**, and more, covering Swiss cities and rural areas.

Swiss Travel Pass: If you're traveling extensively by public transport, the **Swiss Travel Pass app** gives you access to unlimited travel across the Swiss Travel System, including **trains, boats, trams**, and **buses**.

2. Maps and Navigation

Google Maps: Reliable for getting around major cities and hiking routes. It provides accurate **walking, driving**, and **public transportation directions**.

Komoot: An excellent app for outdoor lovers. It helps you plan **hiking, mountain biking**, and **cycling** routes in Switzerland, including specific trails in the Swiss Alps.

Citymapper: A great app for navigating cities like Zurich and Geneva, offering real-time public transport info and alternative routes.

3. Currency and Banking

Revolut: A **global money management app** that lets you store multiple currencies, exchange money at competitive rates, and track your spending. It's great for managing expenses when traveling abroad.

Wise (formerly TransferWise): Wise is an app that allows you to make **international money transfers** with low fees, or withdraw local currency at competitive exchange rates.

4. Local Food and Dining

TripAdvisor: Great for checking **restaurant reviews**, **hotel ratings**, and suggestions for activities in your current location.

TheFork: If you're looking for dining options in Swiss cities, **TheFork** provides a variety of **restaurant recommendations**, along with the option to book reservations.

Michelin Guide: If you're seeking high-end dining, download the **Michelin Guide** app for **starred restaurants**, gourmet options, and exceptional food experiences in Switzerland.

5. Outdoor and Adventure

Outdooractive: Perfect for adventure travelers, this app provides detailed maps and guides for **hiking, skiing, and cycling** throughout Switzerland, including some remote areas.

Switzerland Tourism: The official app by Switzerland Tourism provides an **interactive map** of attractions, festivals, and seasonal itineraries, along with recommendations for activities across the country.

6. Language Assistance

Duolingo: A great way to brush up on your basic German, French, or Italian skills before your trip (especially useful for **Swiss German**).

Google Translate: Excellent for **translating signs**, menus, or conversations when you need help understanding **French**, **German**, **Italian**, or **Romansh** in Switzerland.

7. Weather and Alerts

MeteoSwiss: For up-to-date weather reports and forecasts, especially in mountainous regions where conditions can change quickly. The app provides detailed information on **temperature**, **precipitation**, and **snowfall**.

WeatherPro: Another reliable app for weather forecasts in Switzerland, providing **hourly and 7-day forecasts**, great for travelers planning outdoor activities.

Final Tips for Connectivity:

Local SIM cards are a great choice for travelers who want to avoid high roaming charges. Be sure to compare available plans to choose the best one for your data needs.

Free Wi-Fi is available in most cities and tourist areas, but don't rely solely on it for navigation or important transactions—**download offline maps** and apps where possible.

Battery management is important. Always carry a **power bank** when using your smartphone for navigation or other essential tasks during your travels.

Emergency Numbers & Contacts

Switzerland is a safe and well-organized country with excellent emergency services. It's important to know the emergency contact numbers before you arrive, so you're prepared in case of an unexpected situation.

Emergency Numbers in Switzerland

General Emergency Number: 112

This is the **EU-wide emergency number** and can be dialed for all emergencies, including police, fire, and medical emergencies. It works throughout Switzerland.

Medical Emergency (Ambulance): 144

For medical emergencies, accidents, or if you need an ambulance, dial **144** for immediate help.

Police Emergency: 117

For urgent police assistance or if you witness a crime or accident, dial **117**.

Fire Emergency: 118

In the event of a fire, dial **118** to reach the fire department.

Mountain Rescue: 1414

If you are hiking or engaging in mountain sports and need **mountain rescue**, dial **1414** for Swiss Alpine Rescue.

Swiss Poison Control: 145

If you or someone else has been poisoned or exposed to harmful substances, dial **145**.

Non-Emergency Numbers

Tourist Information: You can call the Swiss tourist information hotline at **+41 900 700 700** for general travel queries, accommodation, and tourism-related questions.

Embassies and Consulates: Make sure to have the contact information for your country's embassy or consulate in Switzerland in case of lost passports or other travel-related issues. Most embassies are located in **Zurich**, **Geneva**, and **Bern**.

Swiss Etiquette and Dos & Don'ts

Switzerland is known for its punctuality, politeness, and orderliness. To ensure a smooth and respectful visit, it's important to follow Swiss social norms and understand local customs.

1. Punctuality

Do: **Be punctual**—Switzerland is a country that values punctuality, especially for business meetings, appointments, and public transportation. If you're meeting someone or attending an event, always arrive on time, or even a few minutes early.

Don't: **Be late**—Being late is considered disrespectful. If you are running late for a meeting, make sure to **apologize** and inform the person you're meeting.

2. Greetings and Social Interactions

Do: When greeting someone, use a **firm handshake** while maintaining eye contact. If you're meeting someone for the first time, it's common to address them using **titles** (Mr., Mrs., Dr.) and **last names** until invited to use first names.

Don't: Avoid being overly familiar with strangers too quickly. **Personal space** is highly valued in Switzerland, so don't stand too close to others in public or private settings.

Do: In more formal settings, such as at a business meeting, it's customary to **address people by their professional title**, like "Herr" (Mr.) or "Frau" (Mrs.), unless told otherwise.

3. Tipping and Gratuities

Do: Tipping is generally included in the price of meals and services in Switzerland, but if you want to leave a **tip**, rounding up the bill or leaving a **5-10% tip** is appreciated. In restaurants, **service charges** are usually included in the bill, but it's polite to leave a small additional amount.

Don't: It is **not necessary to leave large tips**, as the Swiss are quite efficient with their pricing.

4. Table Manners

Do: When dining, keep your hands on the table (but not your elbows). **Wait until everyone is served** before starting to eat. If you're invited to someone's home, it's polite to bring a small gift, such as wine or chocolate.

Don't: Avoid talking with your mouth full. **Do not start eating** until the host gives the go-ahead, especially in formal settings.

5. Personal Behavior

Do: **Respect local customs** and be considerate of local traditions. Switzerland places a strong emphasis on **orderliness**, **cleanliness**, and **quietness**.

Don't: **Be overly loud**—Swiss people value calmness in public spaces, such as public transport or restaurants. Loud talking, especially in quiet settings, can be seen as impolite.

6. Public Transportation Etiquette

Do: **Follow rules and regulations** on public transportation. Always validate your ticket before boarding, give up your seat to elderly or disabled passengers, and queue up neatly in line at train stations and bus stops.

Don't: **Talk on the phone loudly** in public areas. It's considered inconsiderate to make loud calls in public places like trams or trains.

7. Smoking and Drinking

Do: **Be mindful of smoking regulations**—Smoking is prohibited in **indoor public places** and many outdoor areas like parks and playgrounds. Always smoke in designated areas.

Don't: It's illegal to drink alcohol in public places in some areas, so **avoid drinking alcohol in public spaces** unless permitted (e.g., designated picnic areas, events).

8. Gifts and Souvenirs

Do: If you're visiting someone's home, it's customary to bring a **small gift** (flowers, wine, or chocolates). Be sure to present it with both hands.

Don't: Avoid giving overly **personal or expensive gifts** to acquaintances. It may make people uncomfortable.

9. Respect for Nature

Do: Switzerland is famous for its natural beauty. Always **respect nature** and wildlife, especially when hiking or walking in national parks or the mountains. Follow marked trails, and leave no trace of your visit.

Don't: **Don't pick plants**, disturb wildlife, or leave trash behind. Littering is strictly forbidden and may lead to hefty fines.

10. Business Etiquette

Do: Swiss business culture is formal and professional. When attending meetings, be **well-prepared** and respect the **hierarchy** in the workplace. Bring a **business card**, and be sure to follow up after meetings.

Don't: Avoid **discussing personal matters** in business settings, as the Swiss tend to keep work and private lives separate.

Switzerland Travel Guide 2025`

Bonus 1: Switzerland on a Budget

How to Travel Switzerland Cheaply

Switzerland is known for its breathtaking landscapes — and its breathtaking prices. But don't let that scare you off. With smart planning and a few insider strategies, you can experience the best of Switzerland without draining your bank account.

1. Use the Swiss Travel Pass Wisely

This all-in-one ticket gives you unlimited travel across trains, buses, boats, and even some mountain excursions. It also grants free or discounted entry to over 500 museums and landmarks. While it might seem pricey upfront, it pays off fast if you plan to move around a lot.

Tip: Compare the cost of point-to-point tickets vs. the pass. If you're visiting multiple regions or cities, the pass usually wins.

2. Travel Off-Peak

Summer and ski season (December–February) are peak travel periods with higher prices. Instead, travel in shoulder seasons — **April to early June** and **September to October**. You'll enjoy fewer crowds, lower rates, and still-beautiful weather.

3. Stay in Budget Accommodations

Skip the luxury resorts. Switzerland has an excellent range of affordable lodging options:

Hostels – Clean, safe, and often located centrally.

Guesthouses & Airbnb – Great for longer stays or traveling in groups.

Farm Stays (Agrotourism) – Unique, local, and often cheaper.

Campgrounds – Many come with modern facilities and mountain views.

4. Shop Smart for Food

Dining out can be expensive, so eat like a local:

Buy groceries at **Coop** or **Migros** supermarkets.

Look for **takeaway counters** or **lunch menus** in restaurants (cheaper than dinner).

Try local bakeries for fresh, affordable snacks.

Fill your water bottle — tap water is clean and free everywhere.

5. Focus on Free & Low-Cost Attractions

Nature is free — and in Switzerland, that's the best part.

Hike scenic trails in Lauterbrunnen, Grindelwald, or Appenzell.

Swim in crystal-clear lakes like Lake Zurich or Lake Geneva.

Visit historic towns like Lucerne and Bern, where walking around is half the fun.

Many museums offer **free days** or **discounted entries** with local cards.

6. Take Slower Scenic Routes

While fast trains are convenient, slower regional trains offer incredible scenery and lower costs.

Example: The **GoldenPass Line** or **Bernina Express** routes (with reservations made early) can give you panoramic views for less.

7. Skip the Souvenir Traps

Instead of pricey souvenirs, bring home Swiss chocolate from a local supermarket or a handmade item from a village market.

Free Attractions & Scenic Spots

Switzerland is nature's luxury suite — and luckily, much of that luxury comes free.

Despite its high cost of living, the country offers an abundance of **free attractions** and **unforgettable scenic locations** that don't cost a single Swiss franc. Whether you're a city wanderer, a mountain lover, or a lakeside stroller, there's a free experience waiting for you.

1. City Walks and Old Towns

Many of Switzerland's historic cities and villages offer free charm at every turn:

Lucerne's Old Town – Cobblestone streets, frescoed buildings, and the famous **Chapel Bridge (Kapellbrücke)** are all freely walkable.

Bern's UNESCO-listed Old Town – Arched medieval arcades, clock towers, and fountains. Don't miss the **Zytglogge Clock Tower** show at the hour.

Zurich's Altstadt – Explore narrow alleys, hidden courtyards, and riverside promenades.

2. Lakeside Escapes

You don't need to pay to enjoy Switzerland's postcard-perfect lakes:

Lake Geneva Promenade – Walk along Montreux or Vevey, both offering incredible views and access to flower-lined paths.

Lake Zurich – Locals love to sunbathe, picnic, or take a dip in the lake — there are **free swimming areas** like *Strandbad Mythenquai*.

Lake Lucerne – Grab a bench at the lakeside and enjoy the dramatic mountain backdrop for free.

3. Panoramic Hikes and Mountain Views

Hiking in Switzerland is not only a national pastime — it's also free.

Lauterbrunnen Valley Walk – A flat, easy path through a valley of 72 waterfalls.

Oeschinensee Lake Hike – From Kandersteg, a hike brings you to a turquoise alpine lake surrounded by cliffs — no ticket required if you skip the gondola.

Harder Kulm Trail (Interlaken) – Skip the funicular and hike to the top for panoramic views of the Eiger, Mönch, and Jungfrau.

4. Free Local Festivals & Events

Many towns host **public festivals, concerts, and open-air markets** throughout the year:

Fête de l'Escalade (Geneva, December) – A historical celebration with parades, music, and free chocolate!

Basel Carnival (Fasnacht) – Switzerland's biggest and most colorful festival. Free to attend, even if you don't join the procession.

Swiss National Day (August 1) – Fireworks and parades are hosted across the country.

5. Public Parks and Natural Reserves

Park im Grünen (Zurich) – Free green escape with art installations and walking paths.

Botanical Gardens (Geneva, Zurich, Bern) – Most are **free entry** and host thousands of plant species.

The Swiss National Park (while not entirely free, some hikes outside the core zone are accessible with no entry fee).

Affordable Eats: Where Locals Dine

Eating well in Switzerland without spending a fortune is possible — if you know where to look. Forget fancy menus and overpriced tourist traps. Instead, eat where **locals eat**, and you'll enjoy authentic Swiss food at much friendlier prices.

1. Supermarkets with Quality Meals

Swiss supermarkets aren't just for groceries — they're a go-to for tasty, affordable meals:

Migros and Coop – Offer hot meals, salads, sandwiches, pastries, and drinks at a fraction of restaurant prices. Look for their **"Take Away" sections** near train stations or city centers.

Denner – Cheaper than Coop and Migros, great for snacks, drinks, and basics.

2. Self-Service Restaurants and Canteens

Manor Department Stores often have **top-floor restaurants** that serve cafeteria-style meals at fair prices — and the views are a bonus.

University Canteens in cities like Zurich, Bern, and Lausanne often welcome non-students and serve hearty meals for CHF 8–12.

3. Local Favorites: Cheap & Tasty

Kebabs, Falafel & Asian Takeaways – Found in almost every town. Filling, fast, and under CHF 10.

Swiss bakeries (Bäckerei, Boulangerie) – Grab a warm pretzel, sandwich, or pastry for an inexpensive, satisfying lunch.

Food trucks & local markets – In cities like Geneva, Lausanne, and Zurich, you'll find rotating stalls serving everything from Thai noodles to handmade crepes.

4. Budget-Friendly Regional Chains

Tibits – Vegetarian buffet with fair pricing by weight. Healthy and delicious.

Holy Cow! – Swiss burger chain known for generous portions and mid-range pricing.

Äss-Bar — Anti-food-waste bakery that sells yesterday's bread and pastries at deep discounts — great for budget-conscious travelers.

5. Drink Tap Water & Skip Bottled Drinks

Switzerland's tap water is among the purest in the world — and there are public fountains everywhere. Bring a reusable bottle and skip bottled drinks to save CHF 3–5 per meal.

6. Lunch Specials Are the Key

If you want a sit-down experience:

Many restaurants offer **"Mittagsmenü" (lunch specials)** from CHF 15–20, including a drink and main course.

Dinner is often double the price — so eat big at lunch, and go light in the evening.

Best Budget Hotels & Hostels

Traveling in Switzerland doesn't mean you have to stay in luxury chalets or five-star hotels. There's a strong network of **budget-friendly accommodation** options that are clean, comfortable, and well-connected — perfect for smart travelers.

1. Swiss Youth Hostels (Jugendherbergen)

This is Switzerland's official youth hostel network — offering **high-quality, well-located** options across the country.

Cities like **Zurich, Lucerne, Interlaken, and Geneva** all have excellent youth hostels.

Clean dorms, private rooms, breakfast included.

Facilities often include kitchens, lounges, and even mountain views.

Top Picks:

Zurich Youth Hostel – Modern, sleek, and 10 minutes from the lake.

Interlaken Youth Hostel – Stunning views, perfect for adventure travelers.

Zermatt Youth Hostel – Incredible views of the Matterhorn at backpacker prices.

Tip: Book early in peak seasons. These are popular and fill up fast.

2. Budget Hotels That Punch Above Their Price

Many 2-star or 3-star hotels in Switzerland maintain **Swiss quality standards** even with modest pricing.

Affordable Hotel Chains:

Ibis Budget – Found in major cities like Basel, Geneva, and Zurich. Clean, reliable, compact.

B&B Hotels – Gaining popularity in Switzerland for affordable, modern rooms.

easyHotel Zurich – Ultra-budget city stays with basic amenities in great locations.

3. Local Guesthouses & B&Bs

Especially in the Alps or countryside, **guesthouses** (*Gasthaus, Pension, or B&B*) provide cozy stays at lower costs.

Usually family-run with breakfast included.

Offers a more authentic, local experience.

Try areas **just outside city centers** or near scenic villages — you'll save more and still be well-connected by public transport.

4. Farm Stays (Agrotourism)

Farm stays are affordable and memorable.

Stay in mountain huts or working farms.

Great for families or slow travelers.

Sites like **MySwitzerland.com** or **Agrotourismus.ch** list trusted hosts.

5. Airbnb and Apartment Rentals

For longer stays or group travel, **Airbnb or Booking.com apartments** can save you money on both accommodation and food (thanks to kitchen access). Look outside city cores for lower rates and use public transport to get around.

How to Maximize the Swiss Travel Pass

The **Swiss Travel Pass** is a powerful tool — but only if you use it strategically. Here's how to get the best bang for your buck.

1. Choose the Right Duration

Offered in **3, 4, 6, 8, and 15-day** options.

Best value if you're covering multiple regions in a short time.

Don't activate it on arrival if you're staying put — save it for travel-heavy days.

Example: Fly into Zurich, explore it on foot on Day 1, then start the pass on Day 2 when you begin longer train journeys.

2. Use It for Expensive Scenic Routes

The pass **fully covers** iconic routes like:

Glacier Express (reservation fee still required)

Bernina Express

GoldenPass Line

Gotthard Panorama Express

Even short segments of these trains are scenic and worthwhile — make the most of them.

3. Max Out the Free Museum Access

Over **500 museums** are included. Top ones to prioritize:

Swiss National Museum (Zurich)

Olympic Museum (Lausanne)

Zentrum Paul Klee (Bern)

Ballenberg Open-Air Museum

Château de Chillon (Montreux)

If you visit 2–3 museums per city, the pass pays off fast.

4. Use It for Boat Cruises and Cable Cars

Included or discounted with the pass:

Lake Geneva, Lake Lucerne, and Lake Thun cruises

Rigi Mountain railway (fully included)

Stoos and Stanserhorn cable cars

Discounted access (25–50%) to Jungfraujoch and Schilthorn

Always check the **Swiss Pass map** for what's covered 100% and what's partially discounted.

5. Travel Spontaneously Without Stress

The Swiss Travel Pass eliminates the need to buy individual tickets — just hop on and go.

Great for day trips, last-minute changes, or exploring small towns.

No need to stand in ticket lines or deal with conversions.

6. Combine with Local Guest Cards

In some regions, you'll still receive **local guest cards** that offer free buses or discounted entry to attractions **on top of** your Swiss Travel Pass.

Switzerland Travel Guide 2025`

Bonus 2: Hidden Gems of Switzerland

Secret Villages with Stunning Views

While places like Zermatt, Interlaken, and Lucerne steal the spotlight, Switzerland is dotted with **lesser-known villages** that offer jaw-dropping landscapes, authentic charm, and a peaceful escape from the crowds. These are the **places locals whisper about** — perfect for those seeking unique experiences and postcard-perfect beauty without tourist chaos.

1. Guarda – The Fairytale Village of Engadin

Located in the Lower Engadin Valley, Guarda is a perfectly preserved **Romansh-speaking village** known for its sunlit alpine views and traditional Engadine houses with intricate sgraffito designs.

Why it's special: A national heritage site with untouched architecture and views over the Inn River valley.

Best for: Culture lovers, hikers, and photographers.

Must-do: Hike the **Guarda–Lavin trail**, and visit the **Schellenursli House**, linked to a beloved Swiss children's story.

2. Iseltwald – The Quiet Beauty on Lake Brienz

Just 10 minutes from Interlaken, Iseltwald is a peaceful lakeside village with **crystal-clear waters** and views that rival anything in the region.

Why it's special: It has a small harbor, traditional chalets, and a fairy-tale castle (*Seeburg*) by the water.

Best for: Lakeside picnics, swimming, kayaking, and slow travel.

Must-do: Walk the **Lake Brienz Panorama Trail** or rent a boat to explore.

3. Vals – Hidden in the Alpine Highlands

Famous for its minimalist thermal spa designed by Peter Zumthor, **Vals** is tucked away in a remote Graubünden valley, surrounded by dramatic peaks and cascading waterfalls.

Why it's special: Untouched natural surroundings, healing hot springs, and stone-roofed houses.

Best for: Wellness lovers, architecture buffs, solitude seekers.

Switzerland Travel Guide 2025`

Must-do: Soak in the **7132 Therme**, then hike the wild trails around **Zervreila Reservoir**.

4. Evolène – A Cultural Secret in Valais

In the French-speaking part of Valais, Evolène offers a slice of traditional alpine life with flower-filled balconies, cows in summer pastures, and snow-capped peaks.

Why it's special: Deep-rooted traditions, locals in folk dress, and views of **Dent Blanche**.

Best for: Cultural immersion, alpine hiking, peaceful retreats.

Must-do: Attend the **Carnival in Evolène**, one of the most unique in Europe, featuring carved wooden masks and folklore parades.

5. Bergün – Alpine Charm on the Albula Line

Set along the UNESCO-listed **Albula Railway**, Bergün is a picturesque village where every chalet looks like it was painted by hand.

Why it's special: Close to the Albula Viaduct, this village is a paradise for rail fans and hikers.

Best for: Scenic train stops, old-world charm, panoramic mountain walks.

Must-do: Ride the **Bernina Express**, stop at Bergün, and walk the **rail trail** through tunnels and over bridges.

6. Quinten – The Car-Free Riviera of Eastern Switzerland

Nestled on the shore of **Lake Walen (Walensee)**, Quinten is accessible only by boat or foot — and its **Mediterranean microclimate** allows grapes, figs, and kiwis to thrive.

Why it's special: Feels like a secret island village, but nestled in the Alps.

Best for: Nature walks, wine tasting, and unplugging.

Must-do: Hike from **Weesen to Quinten**, then relax with a glass of local wine by the lake.

7. Tschlin – Where Time Stands Still

Located high above the Inn River valley near the Austrian border, Tschlin is one of the most **remote and untouched villages** in Switzerland.

Why it's special: It's quiet, beautifully preserved, and has panoramic views in every direction.

Best for: Off-grid explorers, authenticity seekers.

Must-do: Explore the **Tschlin Brewery**, and enjoy a zero-tourist sunset with a 360-degree mountain backdrop.

Off-the-Radar Lakes & Trails

Switzerland is known for its grand lakes and famous trails, but some of the most **breathtaking outdoor experiences** are tucked away in places few travelers reach. These **off-the-radar gems** are perfect for solitude, nature photography, and feeling like you've discovered something magical.

1. Lake Oeschinen (Oeschinensee) – Bernese Oberland

Why it's special: Turquoise alpine lake surrounded by cliffs and glaciers, less crowded than Lake Lucerne or Geneva.

How to get there: Gondola from Kandersteg + 30-minute hike.

What to do: Rowboat rentals, wild swimming, alpine hiking, picnic by the shore.

2. Seealpsee – Appenzell Region

Why it's special: Nestled in the Alpstein massif, this lake feels untouched and cinematic.

How to get there: From Wasserauen, hike 1 hour uphill.

What to do: Grab lunch at the lakeside guesthouse, hike to **Äscher Cliff Restaurant**, or photograph reflections of the Säntis Peak.

3. Lac de Taney – Valais

Why it's special: A remote, high-altitude lake that feels like a secret summer escape.

How to get there: Small mountain road from Vouvry, followed by a 45-minute uphill walk.

What to do: Wildflowers in summer, peaceful swimming, panoramic ridge hikes.

4. Lac Bleu (Blue Lake) – Arolla Region

Why it's special: A tiny glacial lake with electric blue water, surrounded by pine forest.

How to get there: Short, easy hike from La Gouille (Valais).

What to do: Perfect for families, picnics, and quick scenic detours.

5. Greina Plateau – Graubünden/Ticino Border

Why it's special: A remote high plateau with otherworldly beauty, perfect for multi-day trekking.

How to get there: Reachable via long-distance trails like the **Sentiero Alpino Calanca**.

What to do: Backcountry hiking, stargazing, and alpine solitude.

Local Cafés, Markets & Artisan Shops

Switzerland's charm isn't just in its landscapes—it's also in its **warm cafés, lively village markets, and handmade goods** you won't find anywhere else. These spots add flavor, culture, and connection to your trip.

1. Cafés with Local Soul

Forget chains—seek out cafés where locals linger and every cup tells a story.

Café du Gothard (Fribourg): Rustic and full of character, known for its hot chocolate and fondue.

Kafi Freud (Zurich): Tucked near the university, a cozy spot with a literary vibe.

Buvette de la Saletta (Grimentz): Mountainside café with sun terrace and alpine tea.

2. Weekly Village Markets

Markets in Switzerland aren't just about produce — they're windows into local life.

Lucerne Farmers Market (Tues & Sat): On the Reuss River, with fresh cheese, wild herbs, and baked goods.

Vevey Market (Tues & Sat): By Lake Geneva, great for wine, handmade crafts, and local specialties.

Chur Market (Saturday): Oldest town in Switzerland — offers artisan meats, alpine flowers, and natural skincare products.

3. Artisan Shops Worth the Detour

Look beyond souvenirs and explore **craftsmanship rooted in tradition**.

Armailli de Gruyères (Gruyères): Handmade cheese and hand-carved tools.

Schneider's Holzkunst (Appenzell): Wood carving studio producing everything from nativity scenes to custom figurines.

Atelier Passamonti (Lugano): Leather and bookbinding workshop creating custom journals and accessories.

4. Taste Before You Buy:

Many village shops and cafés offer **free samples** or tasting boards — from **alpine honey to dried meats**.

Bring a reusable bag — many Swiss markets charge for plastic, and shopping locally supports the community.

Peaceful Alternatives to Busy Cities

If Zurich, Geneva, or Lucerne feel too hectic or tourist-heavy, there are **calmer, equally charming towns and small cities** that offer rich experiences without the bustle.

1. Solothurn – Switzerland's Baroque Beauty

Why it's special: Often called *the most beautiful Baroque town in Switzerland*, it sits peacefully along the Aare River and combines historical charm with relaxed energy.

What to do: Walk the riverside promenade, explore the **St. Ursen Cathedral**, and enjoy wine at a quiet café.

2. Murten – Lakeside Old Town

Why it's special: A medieval walled town beside Lake Murten with cobblestone alleys, boutique shops, and a friendly bilingual culture (French and German).

What to do: Stroll the ramparts, rent a paddleboat, or attend the **Murten Light Festival** in winter.

3. Schaffhausen – Rhine Falls & Renaissance Streets

Why it's special: While most come to see the powerful **Rhine Falls**, the city itself is a quiet, architecturally rich gem with pastel-painted facades and tranquil squares.

What to do: Visit **Munot Fortress**, wander through vineyards, and dine by the river.

4. Sierre – Gateway to Valais Wines

Why it's special: Less polished than Sion or Lausanne but surrounded by vineyards and alpine views, Sierre is a **hidden base for wine tourism**.

What to do: Take the **Wine Trail** to Salgesch and sample award-winning local wines along the way.

5. Thun – The Calm Cousin of Interlaken

Why it's special: Located on the edge of Lake Thun, this town offers the same mountain views as Interlaken but with **far fewer crowds** and more local charm.

What to do: Explore **Thun Castle**, relax at lake cafés, and shop in the covered riverfront walkways.

Lesser-Known Festivals Worth Attending

Skip the packed international events and opt for these **authentic, small-scale festivals** that celebrate Swiss culture in meaningful, community-rooted ways.

1. Fête de la Chèvre (Goat Festival) – Grimentz (Valais)

When: September

Why it's special: Villagers celebrate the return of their goats from the alpine pastures with parades, cheese tastings, and folk music.

2. Onion Market (Zibelemärit) – Bern

When: Last Monday in November

Why it's special: A one-day event where stalls sell thousands of braided onions, garlic, and local crafts. Street confetti fights and mulled wine make it a quirky favorite.

3. Bellinzona Carnival (Rabadan) – Ticino

When: February

Why it's special: A vibrant mix of costumes, parades, and street food in this Italian-speaking region, without the overwhelming crowds of larger European carnivals.

4. Appenzeller Silvesterchlausen – Urnäsch (Appenzell)

When: January 13 (Old New Year's Eve)

Why it's special: Locals dress in hand-made costumes with giant bells and masks to welcome the new year with haunting chants and ancient alpine tradition.

5. Lugano Estival Jazz – Ticino

When: Early July

Why it's special: A **free open-air jazz and world music festival** with lake views and a friendly, relaxed atmosphere.

Switzerland Travel Guide 2025`

Bonus 3: Swiss Travel Mistakes to Avoid

Most Common Tourist Traps

1. Overpaying at Mountain Restaurants with Mediocre Views

Many visitors are drawn to mountaintop restaurants for the view—but some of the most advertised ones are **overpriced, crowded, and offer average food.**

Avoid:

Restaurants near highly commercialized areas like Jungfraujoch Station or some establishments atop Mount Titlis.

Tourist menus with inflated prices, especially at viewing platforms with attached eateries.

Do Instead:

Pack a picnic or dine at **smaller alpine guesthouses or family-run Berghotels**, where you get better food, real hospitality, and equally stunning views.

2. Falling for "Panoramic Train" Upcharges Without Planning

Panoramic trains like the **Glacier Express** and **Bernina Express** are world-famous, but **booking premium class tickets during cloudy days** or **not reserving seats in advance** can ruin the experience.

Avoid:

Booking the most expensive seats during poor weather or in shoulder seasons with limited visibility.

Assuming all scenic routes require a premium ticket.

Do Instead:

Travel on **the same scenic routes with regular regional trains**, often for much less.

Check weather forecasts and opt for clear-day travel.

Use your **Swiss Travel Pass**, which often covers the base fare—just pay for a reservation if needed.

3. Buying Souvenirs in Tourist-Only Zones

Shops around major attractions like Lucerne's Chapel Bridge or Zurich's Bahnhofstrasse charge **double or triple** for generic souvenirs like magnets, watches, or chocolate.

Avoid:

Tourist-dense areas with "Swiss" items that are mass-produced abroad.

Overpaying for chocolate brands available at supermarkets for a fraction of the cost.

Do Instead:

Buy chocolate from **Migros or Coop supermarkets** (Läderach, Lindt, Frey).

Visit **artisan workshops or local markets** in smaller towns for handcrafted goods.

Seek out **family-owned watch stores** or local distilleries for authentic gifts.

4. Booking Expensive Group Tours for Simple Activities

Many agencies sell walking tours, cheese factory visits, or day hikes at high prices—**often for things you could easily do solo with a map and a bit of planning.**

Avoid:

Paying CHF 200+ for a day trip that just includes public transport and a few photo stops.

Group walking tours of small towns that are easy to explore yourself.

Do Instead:

Use free resources: most cities offer **free walking tour maps** or app-guided routes.

Use your **Swiss Travel Pass** to DIY day trips to Lucerne, Lauterbrunnen, or Gruyères.

Visit **self-guided cheese dairies and chocolate factories**—many have low-cost entry.

5. Staying Only in Major Cities

First-time visitors often spend most of their time in Zurich, Geneva, or Lucerne thinking it's "easier." But these are also the **most expensive and least scenic** parts of the country.

Avoid:

Booking full stays in big cities without exploring the alpine countryside.

Thinking trains between cities are quicker than exploring regional beauty.

Do Instead:

Spend more nights in **mountain villages, lake towns, or rural cantons**—they offer richer experiences and better value.

Use cities as **arrival/departure hubs**, then branch out.

6. Not Using the Swiss Travel Pass Efficiently

Many tourists buy the **Swiss Travel Pass** and then **underuse it** by staying in one city or not taking advantage of all included perks.

Avoid:

Only riding trains without visiting the museums, boats, or cable cars included in the pass.

Buying individual tickets when the pass would've been cheaper.

Do Instead:

Plan your route to maximize all free entries: over 500 museums, scenic trains, boats on lakes like Thun, and cableways like Mount Rigi.

Activate your pass **on high-travel days** and pair it with regional discounts.

Switzerland Travel Guide 2025`

Money-Wasting Mistakes

Switzerland is often labeled one of the most expensive countries in the world—and that reputation is well-earned if you're not careful. Here are some of the most common money-wasting mistakes and how to avoid them:

1. Not Planning for Grocery Options

Many tourists eat every meal in restaurants, not realizing that **eating out can easily cost CHF 25–50 per person per meal**.

Avoid: Dining out for all meals, especially in touristy areas.

Do Instead:

Shop at **Migros**, **Coop**, or **Aldi** supermarkets where you can get sandwiches, salads, fruit, or even warm meals at a fraction of restaurant prices.

Visit **farmers markets** for fresh, affordable local food.

Take advantage of hotel breakfasts and prepare picnic lunches when sightseeing.

2. Currency Exchange at Airports or Tourist Centers

Exchanging cash at airports or popular tourist spots can come with **poor rates and high fees**.

Avoid: Currency exchange booths at train stations or airports.

Do Instead:

Use **ATMs**, which typically offer better exchange rates (check with your bank for fees).

Use a **travel-friendly credit card** with no foreign transaction fees.

Most of Switzerland accepts cards, including public transport ticket machines.

3. Booking Last-Minute Accommodation

Many travelers assume they can wing it and find a hotel or hostel on arrival—but in Switzerland, this often leads to **limited availability or inflated prices**.

Avoid: Booking hotels or hostels on the same day, especially during peak seasons (summer and ski season).

Switzerland Travel Guide 2025`

Do Instead:

Book early to lock in better rates.

Look into **regional guesthouses** or **Airbnb options**, especially in rural areas.

Use booking sites with free cancellation so you can stay flexible while still securing a good deal.

4. Buying Single-Use Train Tickets Instead of Travel Passes

Many tourists buy train tickets trip-by-trip, not realizing how quickly the costs add up.

Avoid: Paying for every single journey out-of-pocket.

Do Instead:

Get a **Swiss Travel Pass** or **Half Fare Card** if you'll be traveling frequently.

Plan your travel days around your pass validity to maximize its value (e.g., all long-distance rides while the pass is active).

Use apps like **SBB Mobile** or **Swiss Travel Guide** to compare fares and check routes.

Transportation Pitfalls

While Swiss public transport is among the best in the world, it's still possible to fall into a few traps that cost you time, money, or comfort. Here's what to watch out for:

1. Not Understanding the Swiss Transport Zones

Some tourists assume that once they're in a city like Zurich or Geneva, they can hop on any train or tram—only to get fined during a ticket inspection.

Avoid: Traveling without a valid ticket or misunderstanding zone boundaries.

Do Instead:

Understand the **zone system** (especially in cities like Zurich and Bern).

Buy the correct **day pass or multiple-ride tickets** for your zone.

Use the **SBB app** to plan and pay for intra-city and intercity transport accurately.

2. Ignoring Timetables and Missed Connections

Switzerland's trains are famously punctual—**but also unforgiving** if you're late. Missing a connection can derail your itinerary.

Avoid: Arriving late to train platforms or relying on assumptions about delays.

Do Instead:

Always be at the platform **a few minutes before departure**.

Use the **SBB app** to check live schedules and platform changes.

Plan your route with **realistic layover times**, especially if you're switching trains in large stations like Zurich HB or Bern.

3. Renting a Car When You Don't Need One

Switzerland's trains and buses reach **even remote mountain villages**, making car rentals unnecessary for most travelers.

Avoid: Renting a car just for convenience—it often comes with **parking headaches, tolls, fuel costs, and high rental rates**.

Do Instead:

Use **public transport**, which is clean, safe, and scenic.

If you're traveling as a group, compare the cost of a car to group passes or regional transport cards.

4. Not Reserving Seats on Scenic Trains

The Glacier Express, Bernina Express, and Gotthard Panorama Express require **seat reservations**, even with a Swiss Travel Pass.

Avoid: Assuming your pass covers everything automatically.

Do Instead:

Book seat reservations in advance, especially in peak seasons.

If you don't want to pay extra, take **local trains on the same routes**—they offer the same views without the fees.

5. Not Checking for Regional Transport Deals

Each Swiss region has its own discount cards or local passes that tourists often miss out on.

Avoid: Ignoring local transport offers and only relying on national passes.

Do Instead:

In areas like Berner Oberland or Ticino, check for **regional cards** (e.g., Berner Oberland Pass, Tell Pass, Ticino Ticket).

These often include buses, boats, funiculars, and cable cars that national passes may not cover.

Cultural Missteps to Avoid

Switzerland is a diverse, multicultural country, and understanding local customs and etiquette is key to having a respectful and enjoyable trip. Here's a rundown of the cultural missteps to watch out for:

1. Ignoring the Multilingual Landscape

Switzerland has four official languages: German, French, Italian, and Romansh. While many people speak English, showing respect for local languages can go a long way.

Avoid:

Speaking only English without trying to engage with basic greetings in the local language.

Assuming that everyone speaks the same language everywhere (German in Zurich, French in Geneva, Italian in Lugano, etc.).

Do Instead:

Learn a few basic phrases like **"Grüezi"** (hello in Swiss German) or **"Bonjour"** (hello in French).

When in Rome (or the Swiss city), use the appropriate language for that region, and locals will appreciate the effort.

2. Being Overly Casual with Punctuality

Switzerland has an **obsession with punctuality**, and being late can be seen as disrespectful.

Avoid:

Showing up late for train departures, appointments, or even casual meetups.

Treating time as flexible or "Swiss-time," where arriving 15 minutes late is acceptable.

Do Instead:

Arrive **on time or early** for trains, appointments, or social gatherings.

If you know you'll be late, always notify the person you're meeting in advance.

3. Disrespecting Quiet Spaces

Swiss culture values **peace and quiet**—whether on public transportation, in restaurants, or in nature. Loud conversations or behavior that disrupts others can be considered rude.

Avoid:

Speaking loudly or being disruptive in public places, including restaurants, hotels, or public transportation.

Playing loud music or engaging in noisy activities near residential areas, especially in rural or mountain regions.

Do Instead:

Keep noise levels down and speak in moderate tones in public spaces.

Respect quiet zones, particularly on trains or in restaurants where others are trying to enjoy their meals or time.

4. Forgetting to Tip Appropriately

While tipping is not mandatory in Switzerland, leaving a small tip is still appreciated for good service.

Avoid:

Leaving no tip at restaurants or for services such as taxis or hotel staff, as this may be seen as a sign of dissatisfaction.

Over-tipping, which can make the situation awkward.

Do Instead:

Round up the bill or leave about **5–10%** if you're happy with the service, especially in restaurants or cafes.

In most cases, the service charge is included, so tipping is discretionary but still a polite gesture.

5. Disrespecting the Environment

Switzerland is known for its **pristine natural environment**, and locals take environmental responsibility seriously.

Avoid:

Littering or leaving waste behind in public places, even in remote areas like hiking trails or mountain viewpoints.

Using plastic products unnecessarily when alternatives are available.

Do Instead:

Dispose of waste responsibly and recycle whenever possible.

Bring a **reusable water bottle** and use refill stations available in most cities and nature spots.

Respect nature by sticking to designated paths and not disturbing wildlife.

6. Ignoring Swiss Neutrality in Political Conversations

Switzerland's **neutral stance** in global politics is a matter of pride. So, discussing sensitive political topics can make locals uncomfortable.

Avoid:

Getting into **political discussions** or asking locals about their opinions on international conflicts, military alliances, or neutrality.

Making assumptions about Swiss perspectives on global issues.

Do Instead:

Stick to **neutral topics**, such as culture, food, nature, or the arts, when talking to locals.

If you want to ask about Swiss politics, approach the subject with care and curiosity.

What to Pack (and What to Leave Behind)

Packing for Switzerland can be tricky due to the country's **variable weather**, from sunny summer days to snowy mountain peaks. Here's a guide on what to bring (and what to skip) to ensure you're prepared.

What to Pack

1. Layered Clothing for Changing Weather

Switzerland's weather can change quickly, especially in the mountains. Bring **layers** that you can add or remove depending on the temperature.

Pack:

Lightweight base layers (t-shirts, long sleeves) for warm days.

A warm sweater or fleece for cooler evenings or higher altitudes.

A waterproof jacket or windbreaker—Swiss weather can be unpredictable, especially in the mountains.

Pants or hiking shorts, depending on your planned activities and the season.

2. Good Walking Shoes or Hiking Boots

Whether you're exploring cities or hiking trails, comfortable shoes are essential for getting around.

Pack:

Comfortable walking shoes for sightseeing in cities.

Sturdy hiking boots if you're planning to do mountain or alpine hiking.

Waterproof shoes for rain or wet terrain.

3. A Daypack for Day Trips

A small backpack is perfect for carrying your essentials on day trips to lakes, mountains, or cities.

Pack:

A compact daypack for hikes, tours, and city explorations.

A refillable water bottle (Switzerland has excellent tap water!).

Sunscreen and sunglasses (especially in the Alps, where the sun can be intense at higher altitudes).

4. Travel Adapters and Chargers

Switzerland uses **Type C** and **Type J plugs**, so don't forget your adapters if you're traveling from abroad.

Pack:

Plug adapters (for European-style outlets).

Chargers for your phone, camera, or other devices, and a portable power bank if you're hiking or traveling in rural areas.

5. Swiss Travel Pass or Rail Tickets

If you're using public transport, having a **Swiss Travel Pass** or tickets ahead of time will make your trip smoother.

Pack:

Swiss Travel Pass (for unlimited travel on trains, buses, and boats) or printed transport tickets.

Your ID or passport (for ticket verification or discounts).

What to Leave Behind

1. Excessive Luggage

Switzerland's efficient public transport system means you'll be moving around a lot, and large suitcases can be cumbersome.

Leave Behind:

Excessive luggage—pack light to make moving through train stations, buses, and hiking trails easier.

Too many clothes—Switzerland has **laundry services** available in most hotels or guesthouses if you need to freshen up your wardrobe.

2. Heavy or Unnecessary Electronics

While Switzerland is tech-friendly, you likely won't need **heavy cameras, drones, or large electronics** unless you have specific plans.

Leave Behind:

Heavy camera gear if you're not a professional photographer.

Drones, as Switzerland has strict drone laws, especially around protected areas and mountains.

3. Uncomfortable Shoes or Sandals

With all the walking and hiking opportunities, uncomfortable shoes will quickly become a burden.

Leave Behind:

Uncomfortable shoes or sandals—if you're unsure, opt for something sturdy and supportive.

4. Expensive Jewelry or Valuables

While Switzerland is one of the safest countries, it's always a good idea to leave valuables at home to avoid the risk of losing them.

Leave Behind:

Expensive jewelry or items that might draw unwanted attention.

Too many credit cards—just one or two should suffice.

Bonus 4: Switzerland Travel Itineraries

Romantic 5-Day Getaway

Day 1: Arrival in Zurich – Explore the City of Romance

Morning:
Arrive in **Zurich**, Switzerland's largest city, which balances a vibrant city atmosphere with scenic beauty. After checking into your hotel, enjoy a leisurely breakfast in one of Zurich's charming cafés, such as **Café Schober** in the Old Town.

Late Morning:

Take a romantic **boat ride on Lake Zurich**. The lake, surrounded by picturesque mountains, offers a tranquil start to your Swiss adventure. You can enjoy panoramic views of the city skyline while sipping coffee or a glass of Swiss wine.

Afternoon:
Wander through Zurich's **Old Town (Altstadt)**, a maze of narrow, cobblestone streets lined with medieval buildings, boutique shops, and galleries. Be sure to stop at **Bahnhofstrasse**, one of the world's most exclusive shopping streets, for a bit of shopping or window browsing.

Evening:
Have a romantic dinner at **Kronenhalle**, an iconic Swiss restaurant known for its luxurious ambiance and classic Swiss dishes. After dinner, take a stroll along the **Limmat River** for a peaceful night walk, or enjoy a cocktail at **Clouds** in the **Prime Tower**, Zurich's tallest building, offering breathtaking views of the city at night.

Day 2: Zurich to Lucerne – Charm by the Lake

Morning:
Take a scenic **train ride** from Zurich to **Lucerne** (about 1 hour). Lucerne is often called the "Swiss Riviera" because of its idyllic location on the shores of Lake Lucerne, surrounded by snow-capped peaks.

Late Morning:

Check into a romantic hotel like **Hotel des Balances**, located in the heart of Lucerne, offering stunning views of the lake and mountains. Then, head out for a **romantic walk along the Chapel Bridge (Kapellbrücke)**, one of the oldest wooden bridges in Europe, adorned with beautiful medieval paintings.

Afternoon:
Take a **cruise on Lake Lucerne**, enjoying the serene beauty of the surrounding mountains and picturesque villages. You can choose a private boat tour for a more intimate experience or hop on one of the regular lake cruises.

Evening:
Dine at the **Restaurant Balances**, located right by the lake, where you can enjoy a gourmet dinner with sweeping views of the water. After dinner, visit the **Lion Monument**, a symbol of Switzerland's pride and history. It's a perfect spot for a quiet moment together before heading back to your hotel.

Day 3: Lucerne to Interlaken – Gateway to the Alps

Morning:
Board the **GoldenPass Line** from Lucerne to Interlaken (about 2 hours). This scenic route offers breathtaking views of the Swiss countryside, charming villages, and beautiful mountain landscapes.

Late Morning:

Upon arrival in **Interlaken**, check into a cozy hotel such as **Hotel Interlaken**, known for its romantic gardens and views of the Jungfrau mountains.

Afternoon:
Head out for a **nature walk in the surrounding countryside**. Interlaken is situated between **Lake Thun** and **Lake Brienz**, and a leisurely stroll around one of these pristine lakes is an ideal romantic afternoon activity.

If you're feeling adventurous, you can opt for a thrilling activity like **paragliding** over the Swiss Alps, offering a once-in-a-lifetime experience that will surely get your adrenaline pumping as you float above the valley below.

Evening:
For dinner, enjoy a traditional Swiss meal at **Restaurant Taverne** or **Husi Bierhaus**, where you can savor hearty dishes like fondue or raclette, paired with regional wines. Afterward, take a peaceful evening walk through **Aare Gorge** or along the lakeside promenade.

Day 4: Interlaken to Zermatt – The Matterhorn Awaits

Morning:
Start your day with an early **train journey** from Interlaken to **Zermatt**, a car-free

resort town nestled at the base of the iconic **Matterhorn** mountain (about 2.5 hours).

Late Morning:

Check into a luxury hotel such as **Hotel Mont Cervin Palace**, which boasts sweeping views of the Matterhorn and offers an exclusive spa for relaxation after a day of exploration.

Afternoon:
Take the **Gornergrat Railway** to the **Gornergrat Summit**, where you'll be treated to **unmatched views of the Matterhorn**. Enjoy a **romantic picnic** on the summit, taking in the dramatic scenery and the majestic alpine peaks around you. If the weather is clear, this will undoubtedly be one of the most memorable moments of your trip.

Evening:
Dine at **Chez Vrony**, a charming mountain restaurant that combines local Swiss cuisine with panoramic views of the Matterhorn. The rustic setting and intimate atmosphere will make for a memorable dinner experience. End your evening by soaking in the quiet, star-filled sky.

Day 5: Zermatt – Relax & Explore

Morning:
Spend your final day in Zermatt relaxing and exploring at your own pace. Take a **leisurely stroll through the village**, which is full of quaint Swiss chalets and shops selling artisan goods.

Late Morning:

Visit the **Matterhorn Museum** to learn about the history of the region and the legendary mountain, or take a relaxing **spa treatment** at your hotel, perfect for unwinding after a few action-packed days.

Afternoon:
If you want to enjoy more of the outdoors, head for the **Klein Matterhorn** (Little Matterhorn) via the **Matterhorn Glacier Paradise**, Europe's highest cable car station. From here, you can walk on the **Glacier** and take in more stunning panoramic views.

Evening:
For your last evening, enjoy a **private dinner** with a view. Book a **private fondue experience** in a secluded mountain hut, where you can enjoy Swiss cheese fondue by candlelight while overlooking the incredible alpine scenery.

Afterward, end your trip with a **nightcap** at a cozy bar in Zermatt, reflecting on the beautiful moments you've shared during your romantic Swiss getaway.

Tips for a Perfect Romantic Getaway

Book Early: Switzerland is popular year-round, especially in ski seasons, so be sure to book hotels and activities well in advance to secure the best spots.

Plan for Downtime: While Switzerland offers many adventure activities, don't forget to include some relaxation time to recharge and simply enjoy each other's company.

Private Experiences: Consider booking private tours or experiences like a private boat ride, a romantic dinner in a mountain hut, or a couples' spa treatment for added intimacy.

Seasonal Considerations: If you're visiting during winter, don't forget to pack warm clothing and check ski resort schedules. During summer, pack light layers for hiking in the mountains and evenings by the lakes.

Family-Friendly Week in the Alps

Switzerland's majestic Alps are the perfect destination for families, offering a mix of outdoor adventures, cultural experiences, and relaxation. A family-friendly itinerary can ensure that everyone from young kids to grandparents can have a memorable time in the stunning Swiss mountains.

Day 1: Arrival in Zurich – City Exploration

Morning:
Arrive in **Zurich** and start your family adventure with a relaxing breakfast at a family-friendly café like **Babu's Bakery & Café**. Zurich offers many child-friendly activities, including the **Zurich Zoo**, which is home to over 360 species of animals. Spend the morning wandering around the zoo and letting the kids interact with animals from all over the world.

Afternoon:
Explore the **Swiss National Museum** for a family-friendly look at Switzerland's history and culture, or head to **Lake Zurich** for a peaceful boat ride. Zurich's pedestrian-friendly Old Town (Altstadt) also has plenty of quirky shops and cafes, making it a great place for a casual stroll.

Evening:
Enjoy a family dinner at **Haus Hiltl**, the oldest vegetarian restaurant in the world. Their extensive buffet offers a variety of options for both adults and kids, making it an ideal choice for families with varied tastes.

Day 2: Zurich to Lucerne – Lakeside Fun & Historic Exploration

Morning:
Take a scenic **train ride** to **Lucerne** (about 1 hour), a picturesque city surrounded by mountains and lakes. Upon arrival, check into a family-friendly hotel such as the **Hotel des Balances**, with great views of Lake Lucerne.

Late Morning:

Visit the **Swiss Museum of Transport**, which is perfect for families. The museum has interactive exhibits on Swiss history, transportation, and communication, featuring old trains, planes, and vintage cars that will engage the entire family.

Afternoon:
Take a **boat ride on Lake Lucerne**. Families can enjoy the tranquil beauty of the lake while taking in views of the surrounding mountains. Alternatively, take the **Pilatus Railway** to Mount Pilatus for a fun day of mountain adventures, including hiking or exploring the famous **Dragon's Path**.

Evening:
Dine at **Restaurant Fritschi**, a family-friendly venue serving Swiss specialties. The restaurant offers a cozy atmosphere, perfect for families to relax after an active day.

Day 3: Lucerne to Interlaken – Outdoor Fun in the Jungfrau Region

Morning:
Travel to **Interlaken** (about 2 hours) and check into your hotel. The town is nestled between **Lake Thun** and **Lake Brienz** with the dramatic backdrop of the

Jungfrau and **Eiger** mountains. It's the ideal base for a family adventure in the Swiss Alps.

Afternoon:
For an exciting day, take the **Schilthorn Piz Gloria Cable Car**, where families can enjoy panoramic views of the Swiss Alps. At the top, there's a rotating restaurant and observation deck that will keep both kids and adults entertained with breathtaking mountain vistas.

For younger kids, consider a more relaxed **boat tour on Lake Thun**. This peaceful ride offers stunning views and a calm environment for the family to enjoy the scenery.

Evening:
Enjoy a relaxed dinner at **Restaurant Taverne** in Interlaken, where you can sample hearty Swiss dishes like fondue and rösti. After dinner, take a family stroll along the lake and enjoy the peaceful mountain views.

Day 4: Jungfraujoch – Top of Europe

Morning:
A day trip to **Jungfraujoch**, the "Top of Europe," is a must for families. Start your morning early and board the **Jungfrau Railway** for a spectacular journey to the highest railway station in Europe. Along the way, the views of the glaciers and alpine peaks will be a thrilling experience for the whole family.

Afternoon:
Once you reach Jungfraujoch, spend the day exploring the ice palace, the viewing platforms, and snow activities like snow tubing or sledding, which are perfect for kids. The **Sphinx Observatory** offers incredible views of the surrounding mountains, and the **Ice Palace** is a wonder of ice sculptures.

Evening:
Head back to Interlaken for a family dinner at **Hotel Interlaken's Restaurant**, where you can enjoy a relaxing meal in a family-friendly atmosphere.

Day 5: Interlaken to Zermatt – Relaxing in the Swiss Alps

Morning:
Take a scenic train ride to **Zermatt** (about 2.5 hours), where you'll be surrounded

by the famous **Matterhorn** mountain. The town is car-free, making it ideal for families with young children.

Afternoon:
In Zermatt, take a ride on the **Gornergrat Railway** for unparalleled views of the Matterhorn and surrounding glaciers. Families can enjoy a peaceful hike or simply relax at the summit with hot chocolate or a family picnic.

Evening:
End your family journey with a special dinner at **Restaurant Zum See**, a charming alpine restaurant in Zermatt offering traditional Swiss dishes. The cozy, rustic setting makes for a memorable final evening in the Swiss Alps.

Food & Wine Lover's Tour

Switzerland offers a perfect blend of world-class cuisine and fine wines, making it an ideal destination for food and wine enthusiasts. This 5-day itinerary is designed to indulge your senses with some of the finest culinary experiences the country has to offer.

Day 1: Arrival in Geneva – Gourmet Beginnings

Morning:
Arrive in **Geneva**, the cosmopolitan city on the shores of **Lake Geneva**, famous for its gourmet dining scene. Start your trip with a leisurely breakfast at **Café du Soleil**, one of the city's oldest and most famous spots.

Late Morning:

Visit the **Caveau des Vins** wine bar to sample some of the region's **local wines**, such as **Chasselas**, the white grape variety grown in the vineyards surrounding the city.

Afternoon:
Explore **Old Town Geneva** and stop by **Buvette des Bains**, a café with beautiful lake views, for a light lunch of Swiss specialties. Don't miss the chance to visit **Maison A. L. Sauter**, a local chocolatier known for producing fine Swiss chocolate.

Evening:
Dine at **Le Jardin** inside the **Beau-Rivage Hotel**, where you can indulge in refined

Switzerland Travel Guide 2025`

dishes made with the finest local ingredients. Pair your meal with a selection from their **extensive wine list**, featuring local and international wines.

Day 2: Geneva to Lausanne – Wine and Cheese Tour

Morning:
Travel to **Lausanne**, known for its rich culinary heritage and proximity to some of Switzerland's finest vineyards (about 40 minutes by train). Start your day with a visit to **Le Comptoir des Vins**, a local wine shop and tasting room offering a wide variety of Swiss wines.

Afternoon:
Take a guided **wine tour** through the **Lavaux Vineyards**, a UNESCO World Heritage site. The terraced vineyards overlook Lake Geneva and offer some of the best panoramic views in the region. Taste a variety of wines, including **Chasselas** and **Pinot Noir**, and enjoy a light **cheese platter**.

Evening:
For dinner, head to **Restaurant de l'Hôtel de Ville** in Crissier, which holds multiple Michelin stars. The chef's tasting menu will take you on a culinary journey of Swiss flavors, perfectly paired with wines from the surrounding vineyards.

Day 3: Lausanne to Bern – Culinary Exploration

Morning:
Arrive in **Bern**, the capital city of Switzerland, known for its medieval architecture and food scene. Enjoy breakfast at a local café, then head to the **Bernese Market** to sample some artisanal Swiss products like cured meats, cheeses, and freshly baked bread.

Afternoon:
Take a stroll through the **Old Town**, a UNESCO World Heritage site, and stop by **Zytglogge**, the famous clock tower. Then, visit **Käppelplatz**, where you can sample **Swiss cheese fondue** at one of the charming restaurants in the area.

Evening:
For dinner, dine at **Restaurant Kornhauskeller**, a stunning cellar restaurant offering traditional Swiss dishes made with fresh, local ingredients. Don't miss the opportunity to sample a Swiss **raclette**, paired with a glass of fine Swiss wine.

Day 4: Bern to Zurich – Swiss Gastronomy and Wine

Morning:
Travel to **Zurich**, the largest city in Switzerland, known for its cosmopolitan atmosphere and rich culinary scene. Begin your day with a visit to **Zurich's Old Town**, where you can stop at **Confiserie Bachmann** to try classic Swiss **chocolates** and pastries.

Afternoon:
Visit the **Zurich Wine Tour**, a guided excursion that will take you through the **Kreis 3 district**, where you'll taste wines from Zurich's local wineries. The tour offers an intimate look at Switzerland's wine culture.

Evening:
Dine at **Restaurant Zeughauskeller**, a traditional Swiss beer hall famous for its sausages and local fare. Pair your meal with one of the excellent Swiss beers available in the region.

Day 5: Zurich to Zermatt – The Matterhorn Experience

Morning:
Take a scenic **train ride** to **Zermatt** and enjoy breakfast at your hotel. Zermatt is known for its upscale dining, with stunning views of the **Matterhorn**.

Afternoon:
In Zermatt, enjoy a **fondue lunch** at a mountain hut or cozy Swiss restaurant, where you can indulge in the country's most famous dish, **cheese fondue**, paired with a local wine such as **Pinot Noir** from the Valais region.

Evening:
For your final dinner, experience the Swiss Alps' gourmet offerings at **Chez Vrony**, a mountain restaurant offering regional specialties, stunning views of the **Matterhorn**, and exquisite wine pairings.

Switzerland Travel Guide 2025`

Adventure Seeker's 7-Day Route

Switzerland is a playground for adventure seekers. From skydiving over the Alps to canyoning in the mountains, this 7-day itinerary offers a perfect balance of thrilling activities and stunning landscapes. Get ready to experience the best of Switzerland's outdoor adventure scene!

Day 1: Arrival in Zurich – Exploring the Urban Outdoors

Morning:
Arrive in **Zurich** and settle into your hotel. Start your adventure with an adrenaline-packed activity right in the city—try **wakeboarding** or **water skiing** on **Lake Zurich**. Alternatively, you can try **rock climbing** at the **Kraftwerk climbing hall**, one of the largest indoor climbing gyms in Europe.

Afternoon:
Take a break and enjoy a leisurely walk through **Zurich's Old Town (Altstadt)**. Then, head to the **Uetliberg Mountain**, where you can hike to the summit for breathtaking views of the city, Lake Zurich, and the Alps.

Evening:
Relax with a casual dinner at **Zeughauskeller**, a traditional Swiss beer hall where you can enjoy local specialties like sausages and hearty Swiss stews.

Day 2: Zurich to Lucerne – Paragliding Over the Lake

Morning:
Take the train to **Lucerne** (about 1 hour). Upon arrival, head straight for the **Mount Pilatus** base. Here, you'll experience the thrill of **paragliding** from the top of Mount Pilatus, where you'll glide above the crystal-clear **Lake Lucerne** and enjoy panoramic views of the Alps. This is an adrenaline rush you won't forget!

Afternoon:
Explore **Lucerne** and its famous landmarks, including the **Chapel Bridge** and **Lion Monument**. Afterward, head to the **Swiss Museum of Transport** for a bit of history and fun exhibitions on travel and transportation.

Evening:
After your exciting day, unwind by enjoying a lakeside dinner at **Restaurant Fritschi**, a cozy, family-friendly spot serving Swiss fare.

Day 3: Lucerne to Interlaken – Canyon Swinging & Skydiving

Morning:
Travel to **Interlaken** (2 hours by train), a town known as the adventure capital of Switzerland. Start your day by visiting **Swiss Adventure Park**, where you can try out **canyon swinging**. This is an extreme sport that involves swinging across a deep gorge, with spectacular views of the surrounding mountains.

Afternoon:
If you're craving more excitement, try **skydiving** over the breathtaking **Eiger, Monch, and Jungfrau mountains**. There's no better way to experience the Alps than by free-falling from 14,000 feet and soaking in the views.

Evening:
After a day filled with adrenaline, have a relaxing dinner at **Restaurant Taverne**, a local favorite offering a wide variety of Swiss dishes and alpine specialties.

Day 4: Interlaken to Grindelwald – Ice Climbing & Hiking

Morning:
Head to **Grindelwald** (about 30 minutes by train). Start your day by **ice climbing** on the glaciers near the town. With an experienced guide, you can try scaling the ice-covered rock faces and experience the Alps in a new way.

Afternoon:
For those who prefer hiking, take the **First Cliff Walk**, a suspension bridge offering amazing views of the surrounding valleys. The **Grindelwald Glacier Gorge** is also nearby, offering a dramatic and scenic hike through alpine terrain.

Evening:
After an active day, have dinner at **Restaurant Belvedere**, known for its Swiss comfort food and stunning views of the surrounding peaks.

Day 5: Grindelwald to Zermatt – Glacier Trekking & Mountain Biking

Morning:
Take the scenic train journey to **Zermatt** (about 3 hours), a mountain town known for the iconic **Matterhorn**. Begin your adventure with a **glacier trekking** experience on the **Theodul Glacier**, which straddles the border between Switzerland and Italy. This guided tour will take you through crevasses, ice caves, and high-altitude terrain.

Afternoon:

For an alternate adventure, rent a **mountain bike** and explore the surrounding trails. Zermatt has a network of biking routes, including some that pass through alpine meadows and offer stunning views of the Matterhorn.

Evening:

Dinner at **Chez Vrony**, a mountain restaurant known for its fondue and incredible Matterhorn views, is the perfect end to an adventurous day.

Day 6: Zermatt to St. Moritz – Skiing & Snowboarding

Morning:

Travel to **St. Moritz** (about 4 hours by train), one of Switzerland's most famous ski resorts. Whether you're a beginner or an expert, the slopes here offer skiing and snowboarding for all levels. Spend the day hitting the slopes at **Corviglia**, one of the best ski areas in Switzerland.

Afternoon:

If you're looking for something more thrilling, try **heli-skiing** in the Engadine Valley. It's an exhilarating experience, and you'll be dropped off on untouched snow for a skiing experience like no other.

Evening:

Enjoy dinner at **Restaurant Chesa Veglia**, one of the oldest and most charming restaurants in St. Moritz, serving local Swiss dishes.

Day 7: St. Moritz to Zurich – Adventure Wrap-Up

Morning:

On your final day, enjoy a relaxed **train ride** back to **Zurich**. Before you head to the airport, stop at the **Uetliberg Mountain** once again for a final panoramic view of the city and surrounding mountains.

Afternoon:

Spend the afternoon shopping for adventure gear and souvenirs in Zurich before preparing for your departure.

The Scenic Photographer's Dream Trip

Switzerland is a photographer's paradise, offering some of the most breathtaking landscapes in the world. From snowy mountain peaks to crystal-clear lakes, this 7-day itinerary is designed to help you capture the most photogenic spots in the country.

Day 1: Arrival in Zurich – Urban Photography

Morning:
Arrive in **Zurich** and check into your hotel. Start with a **photography walking tour** through Zurich's **Old Town**, where you'll find narrow cobblestone streets, colorful buildings, and hidden gems. Don't miss **Bahnhofstrasse**, one of the world's most exclusive shopping streets, where the architectural contrasts will provide unique photo opportunities.

Afternoon:
Head to **Lake Zurich** for some iconic shots of the city against the backdrop of the Alps. Walk along the lake and capture stunning reflections in the calm waters. The **Zurich Zoo** is another excellent spot for photographing wildlife in a lush environment.

Evening:
As the sun sets, head to the **Uetliberg Mountain** for panoramic views of Zurich with the setting sun casting a warm glow over the city. The perfect golden hour photos await.

Day 2: Zurich to Lucerne – Lakeside Photography & Historic Architecture

Morning:
Take a scenic **train ride** to **Lucerne**, a city famous for its lakeside beauty and medieval architecture. Spend the morning capturing shots of the **Chapel Bridge**, one of Switzerland's most iconic landmarks. The **Lion Monument** is another must-photograph site with its poignant history and dramatic sculpture.

Afternoon:
For landscape shots, head to **Mount Pilatus** or **Mount Rigi** for sweeping views of **Lake Lucerne** and the surrounding Alps. The **Rigi** is known as the "Queen of the Mountains," offering some of the most stunning panoramic views in Switzerland.

Evening:
Capture the sunset over **Lake Lucerne** from one of the lakeside cafés, where you can photograph the shimmering water with the mountains in the background.

Day 3: Lucerne to Interlaken – Alpine Wonders

Morning:
Travel to **Interlaken** (2 hours by train), nestled between **Lake Thun** and **Lake Brienz**. The stunning lake views, paired with the surrounding mountains, create some of Switzerland's most scenic shots. **Harder Kulm**, accessible by funicular, provides a perfect vantage point for panoramic photographs of the surrounding mountains and lakes.

Afternoon:
For more adventurous shots, head to **Grindelwald** and **First** for mountain landscapes, alpine meadows, and the stunning **Eiger** north face.

Evening:
Capture the tranquil beauty of **Lake Thun** at sunset, with the quaint villages along its shores.

Day 4: Interlaken to Zermatt – Matterhorn & Mountain Photography

Morning:
Travel to **Zermatt** (2.5 hours by train), the iconic Swiss mountain town. The **Matterhorn** is one of the world's most photographed peaks. Capture the mountain from different angles by taking the **Gornergrat Railway** for stunning views.

Afternoon:
Explore the **Glacier Palace**, where you can photograph the fascinating ice sculptures. For more mountain shots, hike around the **Riffelalp** area to get closer to the Matterhorn and capture it in its full glory.

Evening:
End the day with golden hour shots at the **Matterhorn Glacier**, where the light hits the snow and creates a magical scene.

Day 5: Zermatt to St. Moritz – Engadine Valley Photography

Morning:
Take the scenic train ride to **St. Moritz** (4 hours), passing through the

breathtaking **Engadine Valley**. Photograph the pristine landscapes, snow-covered mountains, and charming villages as you make your way to St. Moritz.

Afternoon:
St. Moritz is famous for its lake and surrounding mountains. Capture **Lake St. Moritz** against the backdrop of the snow-capped peaks.

Evening:
As the sun sets, photograph the village lights reflecting in the lake, with the mountains providing the perfect dramatic backdrop.

Day 6: St. Moritz to Zurich – Alpine Scenery & City Photography

Morning:
Head back to **Zurich** (4 hours by train), taking photos of the stunning Swiss Alps as you travel.

Afternoon:
Explore Zurich's more modern architecture and capture its contrast with the natural beauty surrounding the city.

Evening:
For your final photos, capture **Zurich's skyline at sunset**, with the Alps bathed in golden light.

Day 7: Departure

Spend your final morning revisiting your favorite spots in Zurich for one last shot before you head to the airport.

Switzerland Travel Guide 2025`

Bonus 5: Swiss Phrases for Travelers

Must-Know Words in German, French & Italian

Switzerland is unique in that it has **four national languages**: **German**, **French**, **Italian**, and **Romansh**. The three main languages—German, French, and Italian—are spoken in different regions. Depending on where you're traveling, knowing a few basic phrases can enhance your experience by helping you:

Read signs, menus, and schedules

Order food and drinks with confidence

Ask for help or directions

Build rapport with locals

Even a simple **"thank you"** or **"hello"** in the right language can open doors to more friendly, authentic interactions.

German (Spoken in Zurich, Lucerne, Bern, Basel, Interlaken, Zermatt)

Swiss German is widely spoken, but High German ("Hochdeutsch") is understood and used in writing and formal contexts. Here are some essential phrases in **High German** to get you started:

Basic German Phrases

English	German
Hello	Hallo / Grüezi
Goodbye	Auf Wiedersehen
Please	Bitte
Thank you	Danke
Yes / No	Ja / Nein
Excuse me / Sorry	Entschuldigung
Do you speak English?	Sprechen Sie Englisch?

English	German
How much does it cost?	Wie viel kostet das?
Where is the train station?	Wo ist der Bahnhof?

Tip: In Zurich and Lucerne, "**Grüezi**" is the local greeting. Use it in shops and restaurants to make a great impression.

French (Spoken in Geneva, Lausanne, Montreux, Neuchâtel)

The French-speaking region is known as **Romandy**, and French here is very similar to standard French, with a slight accent and a polite, formal tone in most situations.

Basic French Phrases

English	French
Hello / Good day	Bonjour
Goodbye	Au revoir
Please	S'il vous plaît
Thank you	Merci
Yes / No	Oui / Non
Excuse me / Sorry	Excusez-moi / Désolé
Do you speak English?	Parlez-vous anglais ?
How much is it?	C'est combien ?
Where is the train station?	Où est la gare ?

Tip: In Geneva, people tend to appreciate politeness. Begin conversations with "Bonjour" and end with "Merci, au revoir."

Italian (Spoken in Lugano, Locarno, Ticino Region)

The Italian spoken in Switzerland is very similar to standard Italian, though with some local flavor and Swiss influence in vocabulary and expressions.

Basic Italian Phrases

English	Italian
Hello	Ciao / Buongiorno
Goodbye	Arrivederci
Please	Per favore
Thank you	Grazie
Yes / No	Sì / No
Excuse me / Sorry	Mi scusi / Mi dispiace
Do you speak English?	Parla inglese?
How much does it cost?	Quanto costa?
Where is the train station?	Dov'è la stazione?

Tip: In Italian-speaking areas, greetings are often warm and expressive. A friendly "Ciao!" works for both hello and goodbye in informal settings.

Language Cheat Sheet for Travelers

Bring a small notepad or save these on your phone. Here are a few useful multi-lingual phrases at a glance:

Phrase	German	French	Italian
Hello	Grüezi	Bonjour	Ciao
Thank you	Danke	Merci	Grazie

Phrase	German	French	Italian
Please	Bitte	S'il vous plaît	Per favore
Yes / No	Ja / Nein	Oui / Non	Sì / No
Excuse me / Sorry	Entschuldigung	Excusez-moi	Mi scusi
Do you speak English?	Sprechen Sie Englisch?	Parlez-vous anglais?	Parla inglese?

Final Tips

Use **Google Translate** or the **Swiss Travel Guide app** for instant translation when needed.

Listen carefully and repeat back phrases—it shows effort, even if your pronunciation isn't perfect.

Always smile. Politeness transcends language.

With just a little effort, you'll feel more at home in any Swiss region—and locals will appreciate your willingness to connect in their language.

How to Order Food & Ask for Directions

Ordering food confidently in a local language can make dining more enjoyable and immersive. Here are the most useful phrases:

German (used in Zurich, Lucerne, Bern, Basel, etc.)

"**Ich hätte gerne...**" – I would like…

"**Die Speisekarte, bitte.**" – The menu, please.

"**Was empfehlen Sie?**" – What do you recommend?

"**Ist das vegetarisch?**" – Is this vegetarian?

"**Die Rechnung, bitte.**" – The bill, please.

French (used in Geneva, Lausanne, Montreux, etc.)

"**Je voudrais...**" – I would like…

"**La carte, s'il vous plaît.**" – The menu, please.

"**Qu'est-ce que vous recommandez ?**" – What do you recommend?

"**C'est végétarien ?**" – Is this vegetarian?

"**L'addition, s'il vous plaît.**" – The bill, please.

Italian (used in Lugano, Locarno, Ticino, etc.)

"**Vorrei...**" – I would like…

"**Il menu, per favore.**" – The menu, please.

"**Cosa consiglia?**" – What do you recommend?

"**È vegetariano?**" – Is it vegetarian?

"**Il conto, per favore.**" – The bill, please.

Quick Tip: In most places, tipping is included in the price, but it's customary to round up or leave a few francs as a kind gesture.

How to Ask for Directions

Knowing how to ask for (and understand) directions is extremely helpful—especially when exploring off-the-beaten-path towns or villages.

German

"Wo ist die Toilette?" – Where is the toilet?

"Wie komme ich zum Bahnhof?" – How do I get to the train station?

"Ist es weit?" – Is it far?

"Ich habe mich verlaufen." – I'm lost.

French

"Où sont les toilettes ?" – Where are the toilets?

"Comment aller à la gare ?" – How do I get to the train station?

"C'est loin ?" – Is it far?

"Je suis perdu(e)." – I'm lost.

Italian

"Dove sono i bagni?" – Where are the bathrooms?

"Come si va alla stazione?" – How do I get to the station?

"È lontano?" – Is it far?

"Mi sono perso/a." – I'm lost.

Tip: Use landmarks (church, lake, square) and point to maps on your phone to aid communication.

Polite Phrases for Better Connections

Being polite and respectful goes a long way in Switzerland. Here are universally appreciated phrases that will help you make better connections with locals.

German

"Guten Morgen / Guten Abend" – Good morning / evening

"Könnten Sie mir helfen?" – Could you help me?

"Es tut mir leid." – I'm sorry.

French

"Bonjour / Bonsoir" – Good morning / evening

"Pourriez-vous m'aider ?" – Could you help me?

"Je suis désolé(e)." – I'm sorry.

Italian

"Buongiorno / Buonasera" – Good morning / evening

"Può aiutarmi, per favore?" – Can you help me, please?

"Mi dispiace." – I'm sorry.

Bonus Tip: Always use formal "you" (Sie in German, vous in French, Lei in Italian) when speaking to strangers—it shows respect.

Switzerland Travel Guide 2025`

Train, Hotel & Restaurant Vocabulary

When traveling in Switzerland, you'll regularly interact with train stations, hotels, and dining spots. Here are essential words and phrases in **German**, **French**, and **Italian** to help you navigate each environment with ease.

Train Station Vocabulary

English	German	French	Italian
Train	Zug	Train	Treno
Station	Bahnhof	Gare	Stazione
Ticket	Fahrkarte / Billet	Billet	Biglietto
Platform	Gleis	Quai	Binario
Departure	Abfahrt	Départ	Partenza
Arrival	Ankunft	Arrivée	Arrivo
Schedule	Fahrplan	Horaire	Orario

Hotel Vocabulary

English	German	French	Italian
Reservation	Reservierung	Réservation	Prenotazione
Room	Zimmer	Chambre	Camera
Key	Schlüssel	Clé	Chiave
Check-in	Einchecken	Enregistrement	Check-in
Check-out	Auschecken	Départ	Check-out
Breakfast	Frühstück	Petit-déjeuner	Colazione
Elevator	Aufzug	Ascenseur	Ascensore

Switzerland Travel Guide 2025`

Restaurant Vocabulary

English	German	French	Italian
Menu	Speisekarte	Menu / Carte	Menu
Table	Tisch	Table	Tavolo
Reservation	Reservierung	Réservation	Prenotazione
Waiter / Waitress	Kellner / Kellnerin	Serveur / Serveuse	Cameriere / Cameriera
Water	Wasser	Eau	Acqua
Wine	Wein	Vin	Vino
Cheers!	Prost!	Santé !	Salute!

Fun Local Expressions Tourists Love

Swiss locals have a charming way of speaking—often blending culture, humor, and region-specific sayings. Learning a few expressions can make your interactions fun and memorable.

Swiss German Expressions

"**Grüezi mitenand!**" – Hello, everyone! (common in the German-speaking region)

"**En guete!**" – Bon appétit! (said before eating)

"**Merci vielmal**" – Thank you very much (a Swiss twist on French and German)

Swiss French Expressions

"**Ça joue !**" – It's all good! (used like "no problem" or "okay")

"**Santé !**" – Cheers!

"**C'est nickel !**" – That's perfect! (literally: it's spotless)

Switzerland Travel Guide 2025`

Swiss Italian Expressions

"Salve!" – A polite, friendly "hello" in formal settings

"Buon viaggio!" – Have a good trip!

"Tutto bene!" – All good!

Bonus Phrase Tourists Love to Use:

"Schoggi" – Swiss German for **chocolate** (use this and watch smiles appear)

"Heidiland" – A nostalgic reference to the Alpine lifestyle (based on the story of *Heidi*)

Final Thought

Speaking like a local—even if it's just one word or two—can transform your travel experience. Locals appreciate the effort and are often more open, helpful, and engaging when visitors make an attempt to connect through language.

Printed in Dunstable, United Kingdom